Sunsets *and* Shooting Stars

a Cape Cod Memoir

Highland Light

RICK SEIDEL, M.D.

Cold Tree Press
Nashville, Tennessee

Library of Congress Control Number: 2007941571

Published by Cold Tree Press
Nashville, Tennessee
www.coldtreepress.com

Printed in the United States of America
ISBN-13: 978-1-58385-218-7
ISBN-10: 1-58385-218-2

To Melanie, Madisen, James, and Jack for the inspiration.
To Mom and Dad for everything else.

—⁓〰⁓—

"Good judgment comes from experience
and experience comes from bad judgment."

—Will Rogers

"Happiness is nothing more than health and a poor memory."

—Albert Schweitzer

"No matter where you go or what you do,
always surround yourself with good people."

—Theodore Woodward, M.D.
Professor Emeritus
University of Maryland School of Medicine

"In medicine, even if you can offer nothing else, always offer kindness."

—Daniel Foster, M.D.
Chairman, Department of Internal Medicine
University of Texas Southwestern Medical School

"The songs are in your eyes,
I see them when you smile."

—Bono, U2
Miracle Drug

—⁓〰⁓—

Acknowledgments

I would like to thank Lynnette Player, Stephanie Woods, Susan Mushinski, Sally Wilcox, and Tommy Gibbon, Jr. for taking the time to read my manuscript and provide insightful and supportive comments.

Lonna Emerson's gifted hands produced the beautiful pencil sketches that represent Cape Cod throughout the book.

Special thanks to Dana Adams PhD, for not only serving as my editor, but also providing me his knowledge, experience, and encouragement throughout this process.

The Pilgrim Monument and Provincetown Museum website was utilized for some of the factual and historical information.

Thanks to Sam Smead (©2007 Sam Smead Photocreative/ www.samsmead.com) for producing the author's photograph.

Table of Contents

Prologue

I begin this prologue with a few proclamations, well, really admissions. I admit that I am not a writer, journalist or publicist. I am a forty year-old physician who is attempting to recreate thirty-five years of memories from a place that seems to exist out of time. A place that has beauty beyond belief, but doesn't seem to care if you notice. A place that allows adventures for the young and peaceful solace for us as we age. An area whose landscape may change dramatically from year to year from winter storms, high wind and waves, but whose change is hardly evident to its annual tenants. In fact, the only dramatic change that we have seen in thirty-five years is the extreme rise in real estate values. Yet there is relatively little development thanks to John F. Kennedy who, in 1961, designated 70% of this area as National Seashore, forever to preserve it in its current condition for generations to enjoy and appreciate—as my family has done for the last four generations. This place is Truro, Massachusetts.

All that I write is true, even if some stories are not believable. The characters in the book are real, and most of them are my family who enjoy this place as I do. I dedicate this to my parents who gave us everything and asked for nothing. Incredible sacrifice in their own lives and marriage has given birth to four successful children and now eight grandchildren. My father is a prominent character in this book. Many of the adventures and mishaps involve him. I don't think I've met a more resourceful person. My father is highly intelligent, hard-working, and diversified in his interests. He can intelligently discuss opera or classical music and quickly transition into world history and politics. His interests are broad and range from woodcarving, guns, fly-tying, and antiques to world history, Salmon fishing, and the stock market. His home, which he personally remodeled himself in the 1970s, is decorated with a flint-lock musket, Tiffany style lampshades, and various wooden bird carvings, all created with his own skilled hands. Fortunate to have managed a company that owned two dairy farms, we spent a great deal of time in the outdoors where he taught us about wildlife, hunting, fishing, trapping, and instilled in me a deep curiosity and love for nature. A person with unlimited interests and potential, he's been only limited in his life by financial constraints, a short temper, and fate. Until age fifty-seven, he was blessed with good health; now a heart condition causes setbacks over the past several years. Including major heart surgery last summer, he has faced these challenges and fought back courageously each time. He has a knack for inviting disaster, but somehow evading it and coming out on top. His friend Guthrie once described him as "a man who carries a bag of black cats over his shoulder, and hopes for the best." Without my father's hard work and passion for this place, this book would never have been written.

Mom plays a more subtle, low-key role in the book, as she does in our family. She is quiet, more a listener than a talker, and served as the organizer and stabilizer in our family. Her compassionate, malleable personality has been the glue that has held our family tight through the years. Mom played a key role in our upbringing, not only working full time at night to contribute financially, but also always ensuring that we were at school on time and made it to all our extracurricular activities. She reinforced Dad's values of hard work, responsibility, and honesty. Many of my own personality traits come from my mother, passed down from her father, Pop Humble. His last name truly befitted him.

My name is Rick Seidel, and I am a gastroenterologist in private practice with five other physicians in East Texas. I have been married to Melanie for thirteen years and have three wonderful children: Madisen, eleven; James, nine; and Jack, fifteen months. As I write, I hear Jack crying in the background as he works on cutting his molars. Madisen and James are both "A" students. Madisen loves to help mom with the baby and plays violin. James is our athlete, starring in soccer, baseball, and basketball. Both kids have an appreciation for summer trips to Cape Cod, which is unique in East Texas, where most kids spend summers on the beaches of the Texas Gulf coast or Florida panhandle.

I am not a writer. I have published many scientific papers and even book chapters throughout my career, all of which have to do with science and medicine, two subjects that have always been my passion. I've never kept a diary or written for the sheer enjoyment of writing, and I may not do this again. But I feel compelled to share my adventures on Cape Cod with others, particularly my wife and family, as we now prepare to build a summer home in this wonderful place.

I hope that you enjoy reading about our family adventures on Cape Cod and may in some way relate to these in your own memories from summer vacations past. It seems as though no matter where we start or ultimately finish in life, many of the experiences along the way share common ground. Everyone understands what it means to enjoy ice cream, it's just the flavors that change.

Sunsets *and* Shooting Stars

a Cape Cod Memoir

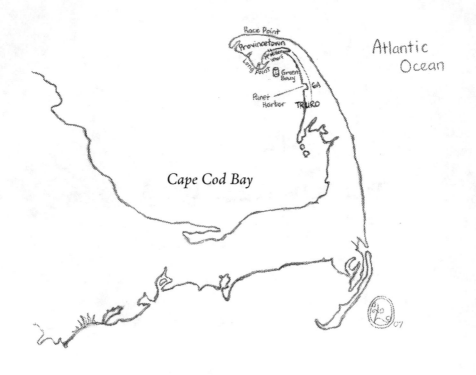

Atlantic Ocean

Race Point

Provincetown

Long Point

Green Bury

Pamet Harbor

TRURO

Cape Cod Bay

Dad's truck

Chapter One

Getting There

It was mid-July, 1985, when I found myself in Brooklyn, sitting on a park bench on a small sliver of grass separating the Belt Parkway from the Lower New York Bay. I stared off to the west and watched the hazy sun disappear behind the brick and mortar of Staten Island. Having just completed my freshman year in college, I was contemplating a career in medicine. I was participating in a summer externship program at New York University Hospital, spending June and July dorming in a Brooklyn apartment with a family friend. With only a couple more weeks until completion, I had confirmed my desire to enter medicine. I also came to the realization that fast-paced city life was not for me and longed for open green areas and fresh air. The time was now 8:30 P.M., and within a few short hours my family would be departing from Northeastern Pennsylvania on their annual overnight journey to Cape Cod, Massachusetts.

I, for the first time in 15 years, would not join them.

As the sky's color changed from violet to black, the stars began to appear, although from this location their radiance was dimmed by the immense glow of the city. I knew that within twenty-four hours my family would be enjoying spectacular sunsets over Cape Cod Bay and gazing upward into the pitch-black darkness to witness shooting stars falling from the sky.

Truro is not an easy destination to reach from Northeastern Pennsylvania where I grew up and especially not from Los Angeles or East Texas, where my brother and I now live. But despite the miles and inconvenience, we keep coming back year after year, more often in recent years. There is something that energizes my brain when I first get out of the car and that initial scent of humid, salt air enters my nostrils and lights up my olfactory lobe. It's a euphoric experience, especially when combined with sun and a good weather forecast for the week. Nirvana is achieved when all of this occurs *and* the fishing reports are good. My mode of traveling to Cape Cod differs now that I rely on airplanes, rental cars, and sometimes ferries from Boston to Provincetown. But the end result is the same: I arrive tired from a long journey, looking forward to a relaxing week ahead. In my younger days, the trip to the Cape was the same every year and actually began months before vacation started.

I was raised in a very middle class neighborhood in Northeastern Pennsylvania and had no friends that I would consider *wealthy*. Most of my friends spent summer vacation in the local schoolyards playing wiffle ball or basketball. Many days were spent fishing in the Susquehanna River, which flowed a few blocks from my house. The fortunate kids obtained a summer badge to the West Pittston Pool; this served as a cooling trough to relieve the relentless heat and humidity. In late July, band camp occupied the remaining days of my high school summers until school resumed in late August. By the end of summer, most of my closest friends had not vacationed anywhere. They would anxiously await my triumphant return from the Cape with stories of huge blue-fish, stripers, and even giant sand sharks that would "bite off your arm as soon as look at you," as my dad says. Color photographs taken with my Kodak Instamatic camera documented these adventures, including my catch. I shared stories of the shooting stars I saw every night as the "water monkeys" crept out of the ocean in search of bad little boys, and I told of the endless lobsters and gallons of clam chowder we consumed during the week.

In Mom's preparation for our summer vacation, she always bought my brother Rob and me matching beach outfits. Although we were two years apart and looked nothing alike, Mom often chose to dress us as if we were identical twins until I was about twelve years old. This same tradition applied to my younger sisters as well—both two years apart and barely recognizable as siblings, let alone identical twins. We would also be provided our yearly pair of brand new sneakers (a.k.a. tennis shoes)—Converse All Stars—prior to vacation. To this day, my instincts are to purchase a new pair of shoes before summer vacation.

With the good come the bad, and the only thing that was purchased for me before vacation that I did not look forward to or willingly accept, was my pre-vacation haircut (and sometimes pre-vacation *haircuts*). By early August my hair had grown long, not having been cut since Easter, and Mom felt that my summer pre-vacation haircut needed to last until Thanksgiving. In my middle-school years, the *shag* look was in style, and we proudly combed our hair straight down on all sides to cover our eyebrows, ears, and curl over our shoulders in the back.

"Make sure you tell Louie to give you a real haircut, not just a trim. I'm paying him good money to give you a man's haircut, so when you return, you better look like you've had a haircut," Mom warned as I exited the kitchen and hopped on my bike.

I pedaled over uneven slate sidewalks, pushed up from the ground by the tunneling roots of century-old silver maple and oak trees that lined our street. While the uneven sidewalks could present a danger to unwary pedestrians, they served as miniature Evel Knievel ramps for the kids on bicycles in the neighborhood.

Louie Biscotta's barber shop was located on the corner across from our school, about four blocks from my house. Louie was the local barber and also school board member, knowing all the kids in the neighborhood as well as their parents; he was well-informed. His brother Frankie owned the local bar and pizza parlor next door. Both Louie and Frankie were served by my morning paper route and were by far the best tippers of my seventy-five customers. Louie would only serve me as *his* customer once during the summer, always before summer vacation.

I pulled in front of the barber shop, let my bike rest against a horse-chestnut tree, and walked into the shop head hung low as if I were entering the dentist's office. The shop was old. Red and white vinyl chairs with steel arms and legs lined the tobacco-stained walls, which were covered with old black and white photos of the Tuscan countryside from where the Biscotta family had emigrated. Large Italian and American flags hung from wooden poles in the corners of the room. Black and white linoleum tile covered the floor, which was dirty, cracked, and cluttered with hair trimmings.

"Well hello there Ricky, you must be getting ready for vacation if you're here for a haircut. How much do we need to take off?" he asked as he pumped up his barber chair and secured the drape tightly around my neck.

"Mom said you can leave it half-way down the ear, trim-up the bangs, and leave the length in the back," I stuttered with fingers crossed behind my back.

"Are you sure? The last few times I heard that, Mom sent you right back over here for more work."

Louie followed my instructions and received his four dollars, after he powdered the back of my neck with his asphyxiating talc. I shook my head to release the clippings as I exited his shop.

"Make sure you keep my newspaper dry, and I'll probably see you later," he laughed as he lit a Paul Mall cigarette in between customers.

I returned home to find Mom unloading brown paper bags of groceries. She instructed me to stand still and walked 360 degrees around my motionless body, inspecting Louie's work.

"Ricky, I thought I told you to get a haircut."

"I did Mom."

"It's not short enough."

"But, Mom!"

"No *buts* mister. You get yourself back over to Louie and have him give you a real haircut. I want it over the ears, short in the back, and get rid of those bangs. Don't come home unless that hair is cut. The next time I'll have your father give you a haircut with his electric razor!"

As I slowly dragged myself back into Louie's barber shop he smiled.

"Back so soon?"

"No comment," I replied as I slumped back down into Louie's chair.

As I said, vacation preparation began months before the trip. In order to provide us a vacation, my parents had to work and save for the trip. My mother worked the evening shift 3:00 P.M. to 11:00 P.M. in the admissions department of the local hospital. My father was a businessman, working as an accountant for a small family-owned company. Despite two incomes supporting our family of six, times were tough, and I'm sure my parents found it difficult to make ends meet. So, my father often worked after *work*, particularly in the spring and summer, doing what he called "side jobs" to earn extra cash to support his family's vacation habit. He did many carpentry and painting jobs for customers and friends around the neighborhood, keeping him out late many weeknights as well as most Saturdays and Sundays. I sometimes went with him to help, but would much rather play in a little league game or go carp fishing instead. He always asked if I wanted to go and help him, but it was never expected. I suspect that he too would rather see me playing sports and doing homework rather than "helping" him do work that would likely make his job take longer to complete. I recall him returning from his second job—many evenings sweaty and covered in paint chips and sawdust—to reheat his dinner and drink a couple cold Rolling Rock beers.

"Just think, Ricky, two more weeks until we're headin' up to the Cape."

"I know Dad, I can't wait! You think we'll catch some big blues this year?"

"Ricky, like I've said before, if I didn't think we're going to catch any fish, I wouldn't bother to go. Did you get you're homework done? Was Robbie tormenting your sisters again? I'm going to put a tin ear on him." My brother was notorious for antagonizing people, especially his siblings. A "tin ear" was a firm pinch and twist on the outer ear, which was more painful than a hair pull and served as an effective threat to induce calm when we were acting out. Other threats such as "the belt," "the shoe," or "wait 'til your father gets home" were also effective, idle threats that rarely resulted in physical action. More than six feet tall and overweight, Dad was an imposing figure compared to our toothpick frames and, therefore, Rob and I would never tempt fate, always taking the threat seriously and calming down, if only for a short while. Back then Dad was a serious man when it came to discipline. Raising his voice much more often than his hand, he rarely spanked us. The simple message given by the firm grasp of his huge hand around our upper arm or the loud snap made by his leather belt as he removed it from his waist was enough to get our attention.

My father was a businessman and left the house every morning clean-shaven, hair always cut short and parted on the side, smelling of Old Spice aftershave. While he departed every morning in a suit, wearing winged-tipped shoes, he often returned home well after dark, now with his suit and tie on a hanger, dressed in a dirty white tee-shirt and paint-stained work pants.

The side jobs continued until the very day we left. I recall many times Mom practically pulling Dad off his thirty-six-foot ladder the night we would leave for the Cape. Typically Dad would work until about seven or eight on Friday evening, eat when he got home, and then load the entire pick-up truck and boat with all of our gear. Suitcases, coolers, fishing gear, tackle boxes, groceries, beach gear all had to be strategically packed by weight and location. The items that would hold up to cold and rain were packed in the boat, a fourteen-foot open Glasstron fishing boat with an old forty-horsepower Johnson outboard motor. Dad greased the ball bearings on the boat trailer wheels prior to loading. We loaded the heaviest items directly over the axles for better stability and stored the more fragile items in the bed of our pick-up truck, a 1967 GMC four-wheel drive farm truck with about 140,000 miles on it when the odometer stopped working. Dad had purchased his truck from a local farmer and used it not only as his means of transportation to and from work, but also to haul firewood, transport animal carcasses that he had trapped in winter or shot during hunting season, and haul the construction tools and equipment he used to do his side jobs. Burnt orange in color, with several dents over the body, cancer eroding the fenders, and a cracked windshield, Dad's truck proudly displayed a brand new brown and white fiberglass cap to keep his cargo, and children, dry. The cab inside was as you would expect from an old farm truck. A sweet aroma of alfalfa and cow manure permeated the air. The passenger side window crank was broken, and there was no knob on the stick shift, just a bare metal rod rising from the floor. The rubber pads on the brake and clutch pedals were worn down to the metal. The back sides of the black sun visors were faded and dusty. Opening the glove compartment door required not only pressing the silver metal button, but also striking the dash firmly to allow it to pop open. The seat was worn and split in many areas, showing the foam padding inside, now covered with an old army blanket tightly wrapped and tucked under and behind the seat, but always needing adjustment. The knobby tires were balding, treads exposed.

The horn didn't work.

Had this truck been owned by anyone else at that time, Dad would have laughingly referred to them as a "hootnanny," which was his 1970s term for a redneck.

I remember being with my father at the local garage/body shop when he was having the truck undergo its yearly inspection and registration. This was long before emissions testing, as the fumes released from the exhaust pipe on this truck would certainly be off the scale and may still be contributing to global warming today. The mechanic was, however, required to check basic functionalities such as the brakes, lights, horn, etc. When Dad was asked to press on the horn, he looked over at the mechanic, who was also a friend, winked, and replied "Beep,beep."

"You told me you were going to have that horn fixed last year, Richard."

"I know, Gus. I've just had a lot goin' on. It slipped my mind. Besides, I only drive this truck around town and out in the woods, nothin' more." Dad looked over at me and winked again, signaling that he was telling a white lie and that I should remain silent, but if asked, I should corroborate his story.

"Is that right young man? You guys ain't takin' this truck out on no highway are ya'?" Gus, wearing an old dirty blue Sunoco shirt with sleeves rolled up to the elbows, looked at me with a toothless grin, his hands and face black with oil and grit.

"No sir," I responded.

"Good. Then I'll pass you again this year Rich, but I want that horn fixed next time I look under this hood. Deal?"

"Deal, Gus. Thanks for your patience. Here's a little somethin' for your trouble." Dad handed Gus a five dollar bill and backed his truck out of the garage.

Finally, when all the vacation gear was packed, Dad placed a piece of plywood over the luggage, which was then covered with blankets and served as a perch for us four kids, packed side by side like in a can of sardines, with very little headroom. The floor boards on the bed of the truck were literally that: old wooden planks of wood with two-inch gaps through which we could observe the asphalt below and through which we were inundated with the fumes of burning oil from the old, worn-out farm truck engine. Dad made us crack the side windows in the cap of the pickup for proper ventilation. He wasn't a scientist, but he understood the implications of carbon monoxide poisoning. The bumpers were made of old, wooden two-by-sixes that were tied to the frame with rope, the front bumper only to be lost on one of our midnight runs to the Cape. After all was loaded, Dad lifted the heavy iron tailgate and slammed it shut. He secured its latches on either side with two S-hooks attached to clanky chains, several links frozen with rust.

At about 10:00 P.M. my father, now drenched with sweat and irritable, would retire to the upstairs bathroom for a well-deserved and relaxing bath. This would be his first of the week and last before we returned from vacation one or two weeks later. My father's approach to bathing was like his approach to church on Sunday: "once a week whether you need it or not." After a hot bath and a clean shave, he laid down for a quick one or two-hour power nap. Mom tried to keep us kids quiet during Dad's nap, although he slept soundly, and woke him at about 1:00 A.M. Most families start their summer vacation bright and early on Saturday morning, lifting off at first light and stopping for a nice leisurely breakfast on the road. Not my father.

"We have to be through Buzzards Bay by 8:00 A.M. or we'll be stuck in traffic all day!"

My father is right on this point, no question. Once you cross the Bourne Bridge over the Cape Cod Canal and actually enter Cape Cod proper, you are served by a two-lane road that connects the town of Sandwich with Provincetown. Sixty-six miles of bumper-to-bumper traffic (if you are lucky and there are no accidents) exists from about 8:00 A.M. until about 3:00 P.M. If you miscalculate the arrival, you are "screwed," as my dad said.

My parents made that mistake once, maybe twice. I believe they also had the misfortune of having the car overheat on Highway 6 under the August sun in the middle of the traffic jam on the way from Sandwich to Provincetown. That is why we always left at night, usually by 2:00 A.M. to break through Buzzards Bay by 8:00 A.M. and avoid the "nightmare on 6." To this day, my father leaves in the middle of the night for the same reasons. Unfortunately, the realtors don't allow us to check in to the rental homes before 2:00 P.M. So arriving at 9:00 A.M. after driving all night to avoid traffic means that you wait all day to check-in, just to sleep off the exhaustion from driving all night. Aside from my father, the other members of my family who still drive themselves from Pennsylvania have now realized that it is possible to sleep all night on Friday, leave early in the morning on Saturday, stop for a leisurely breakfast, and arrive on the Cape just as the traffic is breaking up in the afternoon—no worse for the wear, and well rested.

The all-night drive to the Cape was always interesting. As I stated before, we kids were packed side-by-side on top of a piece of plywood with blankets and pillows to keep us safe and comfortable. My two younger sisters, Kristen and Kim, were strategically placed in between my brother, Rob, and me for fear that we would kill each other by sunrise. The problem was that whoever lay next to my brother would surely be tortured for the entire eight hours of the trip, and my sisters were too little to fight back. Their only means of defense was screaming at the top of their lungs in an effort to shatter the glass that separated our chamber from the driver's compartment. If my father was made aware of the circus in the back of the truck, he would surely turn to us and yell, "Stop the happy horseshit," or "Don't make me come back there!" Idle threats, but threats nonetheless to draw a ceasefire and induce calm, even if only for a few minutes.

My mother served as copilot for the trip. It was her job to stay awake and talk to my father for eight hours to prevent him from falling asleep at the wheel, which as far as I know he never did. I'm sure he had many close calls, as anyone would, especially after working for sixteen hours prior to leaving. We often faced heavy rains and dense fog en route through the night. When my father got tired he would describe "pink elephants" in the road. I never knew what he meant until I worked at UPS during my senior year of college. I loaded five brown trucks from 3:30 A.M. to 8:00 A.M. every morning before class. There were many times I was so tired I saw those "pink elephants" in the road, which are created by hazy red taillights reflecting in tired eyes.

Yes, my mother served as copilot. Mom's problem was an inability to resist her own circadian rhythms and usually within ten miles from home, we saw the back of Mom's head bobbing and weaving through the rear window until finally she was down for the count, her head cocked over at a ninety-degree angle to her neck. It amazes me to this day that she has no cervical disc problems related to her failing to perform her duties as copilot on our midnight missions to the Cape. My father, on the other hand, performed admirably. He simply fought off the Sandman every year with a cup of coffee in one hand and the cool night air blowing on his face through his open window. He had no air conditioner and no radio in that old GMC truck.

Dad never crashed on the way to or from vacation, as far as I know. I can remember seeing accidents several times along the way where cars were lying along the road. My father's comments were usually the same: "Man, did you see that accident back there? Those poor SOBs were probably decapitated!" If I've seen six accidents over the years, all of them had decapitated victims, or so my father believed. We had one close call when I was probably about fourteen years old. Sometimes we would travel with family friends, Phyllis and Emil. Emil is a close friend and college classmate of my father who has a lot of common interests, but does not take risks or live as dangerously as my father. One year, Emil was in his car following my dad in his old GMC truck pulling his old brown fourteen-foot Glasstron boat packed to the gills with vacation gear. As my father was driving, he noticed Emil flashing his high beams on and off to get his attention. I think this was one of those times when Dad was seeing "pink elephants," because unbeknownst to him, the boat trailer tongue had come off the hitch, and the boat and trailer were nearly riding alongside our truck at seventy miles per hour down

Interstate 95 at 4:00 A.M. The trailer was only secured to the truck by the safety chains and sparks were flying everywhere. My father, numb from exhaustion, calmly pulled off to the side of the road without incident. After the metal on the trailer cooled off enough not to burn their hands, Dad and Emil lifted the tongue back onto the boat hitch, secured the lock, and drove off into the night again. And yes, we were through Buzzards Bay by 8:00 A.M.

As I said, my mother was a very poor copilot because she could not stay awake. She did have her children's best interest at heart, especially when it came to her daughters. I think she feared for our safety in the back of Dad's pick-up truck, with gaps in the floorboards, dangerous fumes, and cancer eating through the sidewalls. She also feared for the girls' safety in having to stay in the back of Dad's pick-up truck with two older brothers who were not happy unless they were making at least one of them cry. For this reason, Mom supplied them with some safety equipment: a walkie-talkie to communicate directly with the cockpit, as well as a flashlight to shine through the back window in the event of an emergency. It didn't take Rob and me too long to disrupt their lines of communication by confiscating the batteries from their equipment, or placing pillows in front of the windows to obstruct our parents' view. That is, until the next rest stop when the girls would spill their guts and Dad would threaten us with our lives.

As we traveled all night in the back of the truck, we had no timepieces to keep us updated on our progress. Our sense of time was based on Dad's pit-stops. He always pulled into an all-night diner in Danbury, Connecticut for a fresh cup of coffee and pastry. This was about 145 miles into the trip, and over a third of the way to our destination, where we were allowed to evacuate our crypt and stretch our legs in the parking lot. While Mom went into the diner with the girls, Dad would inspect the trailer hitch, chains, and feel the hubs on the trailer to make sure they weren't getting too hot. He would sometimes climb into the boat to adjust the cargo and secure the boat straps. Mom handed us our provisions for the rest of the night, which included a carton of chocolate milk and a glazed donut. After confirming that no one needed to use the restroom, Dad sent us back into the truck, warning Rob and me not to bother our sisters.

We pulled into a gas station somewhere near Hartford, where we kids usually slept while Dad filled up. Sometimes awoken by the clanging sound of the gas nozzle being placed into and then removed from the tank, it was usually not difficult to fall back to sleep as this marked our half-way point.

When daylight arrived, we could peer out the side windows and get a glimpse of the road below. Our view was limited, but the sight of sand along the side of the black asphalt roadway marked our location on Route 6, and we knew our long journey was nearly done.

When we arrived at our destination in the morning, the kids erupted from the back of the pick-up, clothes wrinkled, hair messed, a little stiff from our plywood bunker, but rejuvenated and energized in anticipation of the week to come. We always stopped for breakfast, where I ordered a ham and cheese omelet and fresh orange juice. It always tasted better on vacation. Mom's tired eyes were lifted as she reapplied makeup from her round, mirrored compact. The family talked about the plans for the week. How soon until we can launch the boat? When can we go raking sand eels for bait? Is it windy enough to fly a kite? When is Dad going to make his clam chowder? Can we go to the top of Pilgrim Monument this year? Do you think the ocean will be too cold to swim? When can we go squiddin' off MacMillan Wharf?

My favorite thing to do when we arrived was to race my brother onto the beach and bury my hands and feet under the soft, warm sand, smell the salt air, and feel the inviting sun and brisk wind on my face. I can't remember ever arriving on the Cape in bad weather. Certainly, we traveled through bad weather— rain and fog—through the night. But I don't remember having a bad first day. This is probably not reality and explainable by our brain's amazing ability to forget or diminish bad memories; however, in my mind it is true. Every year, as far back as I can remember, we arrived in good weather. And to this day, wherever we are staying, I make it a point to first get to the ocean-side, take my shoes off, roll up my blue jeans, and walk out onto the beach.

Sitting there, all four appendages under the warm sand, looking out over the water and listening to the churning, impatient tide with salt wind in my face, I am home.

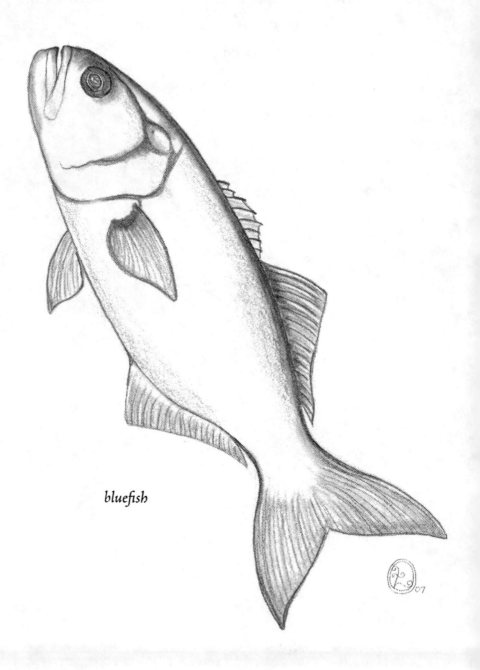

bluefish

Chapter Two

Our Evolving Relationship With the Bluefish

The Bluefish (*Pomatomus saltatrix*) are greenish-blue sturdy fish related to jacks, pompano, and roosterfish. They are noted for their large head and sharp triangular teeth. Their range off the Atlantic coast extends from Nova Scotia to Florida. They migrate northward in the spring and summer and southward in the fall and winter. Bluefish are a pelagic species that travel in large schools of like-sized fish. Bluefish are voracious predators and feed on a variety of fish and invertebrate species and will strike at almost any object in the water column.

The waters off Cape Cod are usually boiling with bluefish by July and August. They are extremely aggressive fish. We have been pursuing this species since our earliest trips to the Cape, mainly because they provide a lot of action and excitement and are dangerous if not taken seriously. By now I consider myself an experienced handler of the bluefish, capable of grasping the toothy, eating machine gently behind the gill plate, extracting the hook and releasing the fish back into the water unharmed and with relatively few scars and no amputated digits thus far. I am quite proud of this skill because many a fisherman has lost a finger or two between the jaws of a bluefish. They have the crushing force of a pit bull.

I can vividly recall my first experience fishing for blues in Cape Cod Bay. I was seven years old, and my father and I were invited to fish in the bay with Chick Mancuso in his twenty-one-foot center-console Boston Whaler. To us, this was the oceanic equivalent of being invited to fly to a Dallas Maverick's game with Mark Cuban in his private Gulfstream. Chick was a long-time Cape Codder, well-respected by the locals for his fishing knowledge. He was thin, but muscular with a dark-brown tan and silver hair. He always wore shorts and boat shoes and was shirtless most of the time. He looked at least twenty years younger than his eighty-two years. Chick seemed to know everything there was to know about bluefish, and we didn't have a clue. In fact, I remember the first bluefish we ever hooked.

We were trolling through a group of terns (seabirds) diving like kamikaze planes from fifty feet above the water, hitting the surface at full throttle, disappearing for a few seconds and then breaking from below with sand eels firmly held in their beaks. This is one of my favorite sights on Cape Cod.

"Always look for the birds," said Chick, "and you will find fish."

This rule holds true today. When you see terns diving for sand eels, they're being chased to the surface by aggressively feeding fish below. As we trolled through the terns on our maiden voyage for blues—dragging a blue and silver Rebel lure behind wire line—the thick trolling rod began to abruptly bounce in the rod holder and the reel began to scream.

"Fish on!" yelled Chick.

He lifted the rod from the rod holder and handed it to my father, up to this point only a very experienced fresh-water angler.

"Holy shit!" yelled my father, "He's taking line, he's taking line! This is no candy-ass fish, Chick! He's pulling my arms off!"

With each statement my father's voice got louder and climbed an octave or two from the excitement. His expressions were similar in times of both joy and anger: loud voice with occasional high-pitched squeals. The huge fish was breaking water behind the boat about a hundred yards back. With each explosion, you could see the white water being whipped to foam and the bright-red gills exposed as the fish shook its massive head trying to spit the hook. Several minutes and several more expletives went by, and my father and the fish both began to tire. "Oh boy, oh boy" were now the only words my father could utter. All this time Chick stood silent except to offer a few words of support to my father.

"Hang in there Rich, you're doin' a good job. I'll have another beer, you're going to be a while. DON'T GET THE LINE WRAPPED AROUND MY PROP!!!!!"

As the fish neared the boat it stayed deep. We could see its silver side and turquoise/green back well through the clear bay water. Its large yellow eye was looking back at us as he made one more effort to tear away from the boat. We still didn't have a clue what we had hooked into.

"What the hell kinda fish are we dealing with here, Chick? This looks like a shark. Maybe I got a small tuna here."

"That's a bluefish," said Chick confidently.

"A what?" asked my father in a voice pitched higher than my seven-year-old vocal cords could produce.

"A bluefish, they're all over the bay. Want to keep him or turn him loose?"

"Keep him! LaVerne and Pop will never believe me if I don't show them. I'm sure Nana will have a recipe."

Holding the wire line in his left hand, Chick sank his large, silver gaff into the side of the bluefish and clubbed it over the head alongside of the boat before bringing it on board. Now motionless, with blood dripping onto the white floor, the fish was dropped into a box, on top of a block of ice.

"Congratulations, Rich, you landed your first bluefish. Hope you enjoy him."

Rule number one: unless you know what you're doing, don't assume anyone can prepare bluefish and don't assume you or any one else will enjoy this oily, dark-meat fish. Rule number two: don't boat a bluefish unless you really know what you are doing, or you've killed the fish prior to bringing it onto the boat. The method of execution, bluefish style, is by means of a small Louisville Slugger baseball bat applied swiftly and aggressively to the fish's forehead. Once the fish has suffered a cerebral contusion and has died, you can then safely bring it aboard and lay it in a cool place, preferably on ice. My father ultimately mastered the bat-to-the-head technique and used it with all the fervor of a starving caveman pursuing his last meal. This technique was soon abandoned after we realized that none of our family members enjoy eating bluefish, and although my father did kill bluefish and place their carcasses in jars to ferment and become fox bait during his years as a trapper, we now practice "catch and release."

We caught many fish that day with Chick and learned many lessons from him and others over the years. We now are the fishermen teaching others about the ways of the bluefish and catch them using many methods. We've caught them on fluke rigs in the harbor using live mummichugs or sand eels. We've caught several blues at one time trolling with umbrella rigs. My absolute favorite technique is throwing surface plugs for aggressively feeding schools of fish. There is nothing more exciting than seeing terns diving, bluefish breaking water, and throwing a large surface plug into that feeding frenzy. As I rapidly retrieve the plug watching it splash over the surface, suddenly the water explodes as several fish lunge at the lure, and the fight is on! The excitement can be infectious and contagious and even downright dangerous.

One summer day my brother Rob and I were out in the bay with Dad on our fourteen-foot Glasstron when the terns came and the water began to boil. Blues were everywhere. Dad was in his captain's chair enjoying an Old Milwaukee and giving us the order.

"Rig up those poppers boys. Work those plugs! They're here." One octave higher he said, "I CAN SMELL 'EM!!!!"

Often, there are so many fish in the school you can actually smell them. I was fourteen and was a fairly experienced plug fisherman by this point. Rob was twelve, and he was not. He was caught up in the moment, almost psychotic with excitement. He had one thing on his mind: hook and land the first bluefish so he could have bragging/tormenting rights and also face a sure promotion up the ladder, perhaps even to first mate, which I currently held. We both hurled our plugs into the water and made them slap the surface on the retrieve. Rob briefly hooked a bluefish, but the hook was spit on the first jump.

"Burn you bubbascubba!" I promptly replied. "Don't think you can out-fish Virgil Ward." *Bubbascubba* was a derogatory word invented by my brother used to harass and humiliate his adversary.

"Screw you slick!" was his reply.

I beat him to the second cast, but his plug never made it back into the water. In the heat of the battle, with all the torquing force that Tiger Woods puts on a full stinger two iron, Rob's plug was launched from the end of his eight-foot surf rod directly into the side of my head, all three treble hooks embedded into my skull. I was initially dazed after being struck with the ten-ounce plug, but quickly realized what had happened and tried to fight back the tears. Rob's initial response was "Dad, you got another plug?"

Dad's initial response: "Holy shit, you stuck a plug in your brother's head! Hey, Ricky, you ok? He didn't get you in the eye, did he?"

My eye was spared by about two inches. Our fishing was over for the day; Rob was demoted to the lowly deck-scrubber rank, which he maintained for several years; and we were off to the local medical clinic to have this eight-inch, bright-orange plug removed from my head—and a tetanus shot to boot.

To this day, I don't eat bluefish. I still love to throw plugs for them and release them unharmed, feeling their power in my grasp. And I strongly recommend that we *troll* for blues when brother Rob is on the boat.

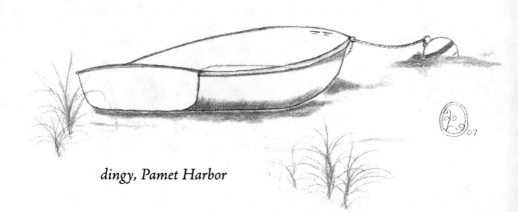

dingy, Pamet Harbor

Chapter Three

Pamet River

Truro is a town of breathtakingly beautiful beaches, old Cape homes, artists' studios, and lighthouses, among many other things. The town is divided from the north and south by Pamet River whose depths rise and fall with the tides, joining bay to ocean as it flows through tall, grassy marshlands. Pamet Harbor rests at the mouth of where the river flows into Cape Cod Bay and is one of the most spectacular sites in Truro. This serene estuary keeps many small vessels safe from high seas and strong winds. Corn Hill rises to the north across a marshland with serpigineous tidal channels, home to oysters, steamer clams, mussels and other various shellfish and crab. The tall marsh grass dances in the winds, which blow unhindered off the open bay to the west. It was here that the Pilgrims wintered in 1620, living off the corn that was stored by the Pamet Indians before leaving the following year for Plymouth across the bay. By the mid 1800s, Pamet Harbor was a major fishing and whaling center, only to be crushed by two major storms in 1841 and 1860, which ultimately crippled Truro's economy.

Pamet Harbor remains my favorite destination on the Cape. To this day, I enjoy driving down Depot Road—lined by quaint old Cape Cod houses with tall hedges and old hardwood trees concealing artist studios and actors' retreats—to enter the parking lot that overlooks the harbor. There are unbelievable views, especially at dusk when the sky changes color dramatically as the sun sets over Provincetown. As the setting sun meets the horizon, the sky becomes a color somewhere between red and yellow on the spectrum, but much more intense and beautiful: something like a tangerine-pink. If you stood there you would know exactly what I mean. Looking down the mouth of the Pamet River toward the bay, beyond the fly fisherman casting Clouser minnows for stripers, you may see large gray clouds forming in the distance but allowing distinct columns of bright yellow sunbeams to connect Heaven to the bay. The contrast of light is always amazing to my untrained eye, and I can only imagine how an artist feels as he translates this beautiful image to canvas.

Pamet Harbor is never crowded and rarely busy. In the summer months, the lot will be lined with pickup trucks and boat trailers parallel with enough room on the perimeter to allow tourists to pass in their cars. Depending on the tide, you will often find fishermen launching and retrieving their boats from the two tandem boat ramps that connect the south side of the parking lot with the west end of Pamet Harbor. Next to the boat ramp is a small shack that houses Swishy, an eighty-four year old Portuguese native who runs the parking lot and the harbor with an iron fist. Swishy has for the town of Truro labored for forty years and has worked his way up the ranks from clam warden to his present position as parking lot superintendent for Pamet Harbor. Swishy, all of five-foot six and about one-hundred twenty pounds, is the first to greet you when you pull into the parking lot looking to launch your boat. He wears an olive-gray uniform with pants held by a cracked leather belt wrapped nearly twice around his skinny waist. His fee is six dollars payable in cash at the time you launch. If you launch when he is not there, you pay him when you retrieve your boat. Either way Swishy gets his money. At first introductions, he strikes you as a very confident and crusty old salt who knows the waters and the fishing well. After years of interactions with Swishy, I've come to realize that he's a crusty old salt with a warm heart who usually delivers the same fishing report year after year. He is very cynical regarding tourists' abilities to navigate their vessel, no matter what the size, and is not very helpful when it comes to anything other than accepting your six dollars and handing you the parking permit.

I don't believe that Swishy was born a cynical salt, but developed into one after years of interactions with arrogant, often drunk, individuals who think they have more knowledge and rights to the area than the next guy. He tells stories of a famous actor who owns a house near the parking lot planning a party one summer weekend. The actor was notifying Swishy that he would be using the parking lot as an overflow area for his guests to park, free of charge. Well, that was all Swishy needed to hear. "You take your fuckin' Mercedes and stay the hell out of my parking lot, or I'll have them towed to the bottom of the bay!"

You don't tempt fate with Swishy. You ask his permission, ask his opinion, and pay him the six dollars.

Swishy is convinced that most recreational fisherman and boaters launching at Pamet Harbor don't know what they are doing. I must admit that he is not too far off the mark. However, in defense of the recreational fisherman, and being one myself, I feel as though I need to make a few brief points before I prove from my family's own experience that what he says is true.

First, we are not true Cape Codders or coastal-living people for that matter and, therefore, are significantly nautically handicapped. My father, Uncle Tom, and Uncle Bob have always been boat owners and fisherman since they were young. We spent many hours angling in Pennsylvania and New York State pursuing fresh-water species on fresh-water bodies of water, primarily small to mid-sized lakes and rivers in small watercraft. When you transfer the same small watercraft to saltwater bays and open ocean, the game changes completely.

In life, the two keys to success are being hardworking and

intelligent. Success can be achieved with only one of these traits if that trait is fully expressed. For example, some lazy people can muddle through life because they have high intelligence. I also know some extremely successful, not so intelligent, but hard-working folks. However, having the "lethal mutation"—being lazy and stupid—is not compatible with success, and the poor soul who inherits both of these traits is unfortunately doomed to failure. In extrapolating this analogy to seamanship on Cape Cod, our family was a heterozygote. We were all intelligent and hardworking, but we were handicapped by small vessels and little experience on the open water.

The waters in the North Atlantic can change as abruptly and severely as the weather, probably more so. I can remember many days when the bay was as placid as an old mill pond, only to become a raging sea as the wind changed direction on a whim. I remember standing on the dock at Pamet Harbor with my father as a storm was blowing in from the Northwest. Two fishermen were approaching the dock in a nineteen-foot center-consol Boston Whaler. They were wearing bright-yellow rubber overalls and rain gear, were red faced, and were beaten by the wind. Their hair was soaking wet, and they stood in ten inches of water filling the bottom of their boat. "Thirty minutes out and three and a half hours to get back" was all they said. You have to respect the waters off of Cape Cod.

For many years we suffered from the small-vessel problem.

Dad, Uncle Bob, and Uncle Tom all brought their boats to the Cape on many summer vacations. We also had many friends bring their boats over the years. It seemed as though there might be safety in numbers out in the bay if the weather turned or someone had mechanical problems. This was a false sense of security—as I'll discuss in future chapters—since having small boats left you much more vulnerable to weather, didn't allow you to get to the best fishing areas, and limited the number of days you could actually launch your boat in the first place.

No matter where we were staying for that week or two in Truro, our morning routine was the same. Dad, Rob, and I would always get to the bay to look for whitecaps, which implied the waves were too large for our small boat to handle. White-caps were just slightly less disappointing than rain. Rain meant staying inside, wrestling with your brother, tormenting your sisters, and probably getting on your parents' nerves, risking Dad's belt across your ass. Rain might mean going shopping in Provincetown or doing tourist activities like visiting museums and lighthouses. Rain, to me, meant boredom and definitely meant no fishing, probably not even from the beach. Whitecaps meant rough seas and, therefore, no fishing in the bay and espe-cially not in the ocean. However, small boats could be launched from the Provincetown boat launch into the harbor, which was protected from the wind and often calm. And that was our approach with small boats; launch from Provincetown, fish for fluke in the harbor and hope for a wind change to allow access to the bay. Small boats are not all bad and do have some advantages. They are easier to tow, easier to launch, and can be beached in an emergency. I wish I could add more to that short list. Would I trade any of my memories of fishing out of a small boat for so many years on Cape Cod? No. Would I trade in my larger boat now for the small boat that created these memories? Not on your life.

Now back to Swishy's point: Most recreational fisherman and boaters don't know what they are doing. We will prove his point many times in this book. After many years in small boats, whether it be our own boat, rental boats from Flyer's Marina, or spending some vacations with no boat, we finally graduated to a big boat. Remembering that all things are relative and one man's shack can be another man's castle, we finally found our yacht. I remember the call as though it was yesterday.

In the spring of 1997, Dad's friend was moving to Alaska and decided to sell his twenty-three-foot Sea Swirl. To us, this boat was unbelievable. A very reliable, sturdy, clean ocean-going vessel powered by a 150-horsepower Johnson Ocean Runner motor. It had very low hours and was kept dry and used exclusively in Lake Erie. Imagine that, a saltwater vessel used only in fresh water. It could not be any more perfect. The boat was white with turquoise trim and accent. A tall, stainless-steel hard-top tower protected the cockpit from the sun. The style was cuddy cabin/walk around, and the bow was bordered by a stainless-steel rail, which led to a small fly bridge protruding off the front. Down below, the cabin would sleep three and housed a small port-o-potty and sink. With a GPS, fishfinder, ship to shore radio, and two live wells, we were equipped to compete with the most seasoned saltwater angler. The price was also right. Dad, Rob, and I each gladly put up $6000 and took this beauty off that poor sucker's hands. Indeed, we now had ourselves a big boat with all the bells and whistles, but still were heterozygotes. We still lacked experience.

After much discussion with friends and family, we decided to name our boat *The Watermonkey*, to honor the creatures so often talked about by my father when we were vacationing on the Cape. Other considerations such as *Race Runner, Deadly Rig, Reel Fun, Willful Crossing*, just didn't seem as appropriate.

Living in Texas, I was unable to help with anything other than the financing of the boat and left the initial maintenance and captaining to Dad and Rob. They quickly had the boat cleaned and waxed and were navigating around Harvey's Lake, a decent-sized freshwater lake in Northeastern Pennsylvania. Dad quickly mastered the controls, which differed greatly from his old four-teen-foot Glasstron. He now had an automatic bilge pump and trim to deal with. The fishfinder was part of the console, not some small tackle box you carried on board. The gas tank was actually part of the boat, not two red metal cans we hauled to and from the boat.

We even had a horn—that worked.

It wasn't long before Dad was buzzing around Harvey's Lake, waving to all of the onlookers who probably had not seen a boat of this size on the lake before. Dad was literally now a big fish on a small pond. With a tight grip on the steering wheel with his left hand, and the throttle with his right, he leaned forward into the wind from his captain's chair. His Orvis cap turned backwards on his head and teeth gritted, he was proud of the huge wake produced by our boat as he sped past helpless victims in smaller boats soon to experience his tsunami, much as he had experienced so many times before.

"Look at those poor suckers over there. They don't know what hit'em." Dad laughed as he looked back to see rowboats and canoes rocking as angry passengers grabbed hold of the rail.

Over the next few months, Dad proudly took other friends and family members out on the lake in his new vessel, like Rodney Dangerfield did in the movie *Caddyshack*. He occasionally allowed others to take the wheel, but always kept close watch and barked out orders if he disagreed with their navigational moves. Dad had reached the top of his game on Harvey's Lake. He even mastered the art of trailering the boat and backing it down the boat ramp with the trailer. This is one of the more difficult maneuvers to master, especially when the rear view is compromised by the boat sitting on top of the trailer. The steering wheel moves are counter-intuitive, and much practice is required.

With months of practice and hours on the lake under his belt, Dad was ready to move to the next level. We were now prepared to introduce our boat to the waters off Cape Cod.

Shiver me timbers, August 1997!

With everyone in our extended family there to witness the maiden voyage of *The Watermonkey*, we pulled triumphantly into Pamet Harbor parking lot. My brother Rob's new champagne Ford F250 four-wheel drive pick-up truck pulled boat and trailer. We drove up to Swishy, who commented on our beautiful rig. Dad was grinning from ear to ear, probably as proud as he felt on the day each of his children were born, for he now owned the means to pursue big fish in bad weather and get out beyond the bay, around the back side of the Cape into the cold, deep waters of the North Atlantic. Places like Race Point, the Washout, Herring Cove, George's Bank, where legends are made catching huge stripers and giant tuna. Dad pulled out his wallet to pay Swishy his six dollars, gave him a ten, and told him to keep the change, because Dad was now a high roller in Pamet Harbor.

Rob carefully and slowly backed the trailer down the ramp, with Dad now positioned inside the boat sitting proudly in his captain's chair, waving to the family and other spectators as he barked out some orders to us. Uncles Bob and Tom guided the trailer back using hand gestures as signals to move to the left or right. Most of the time Uncle Bob would yell "You're good, you're good" or "WHOA, WHOA" as the trailer's wheels entered the water.

Dad would ask "Are you sure the plug's in? We got oil?"

We all agreed that Dad (a.k.a. Captain Dick) would have the honor of moving the boat off the trailer and pulling up along-side the dock while we parked the truck and trailer. Uncle Carl was designated to stand on the dock and steady the boat as Dad pulled alongside. Uncle Tom and I untied the safety rope from the bow ring and unlocked the crank that secured the boat to the trailer. Dad trimmed down the motor slightly and then fired up the engine as an amorphous cloud of carbon smoke rose from the exhaust. We let the motor idle for a couple minutes to warm up as there was no one waiting to launch. With the Captain's order "Let'r go!" uncle Tom and I pushed the boat from its berth on the trailer as Dad pulled back on the throttle and put it into reverse gear. Rob pulled the truck forward, and we all stood and watched as Dad backed away from the boat launch.

Houston, we have a problem.

With all the checking we did before launch, we forgot to release the safety bar that secures the motor and prevents it from trimming all the way down. This was not apparent until Dad tried to lower the motor down farther in deeper water at which time he realized there was no way to control the boat in forward or reverse. My God, what had we done?

Dad was soon making 360-degree circles in reverse in the

harbor screaming, "I can't steer it, I can't steer it!" The wind picked up and began blowing him farther away from the dock and toward the boats moored in the harbor. Dad realized he was in trouble and decided to turn the motor off and give up all control to the wind. He did try to protect the boat by holding rubber cushions in between our boat and the others as they neared each other. My uncles yelled from the shore, "Rich, what the hell are you doing? Drive the boat to the dock!"

"I'm trying, I'm trying!" he yelled back. "The son-of-a-bitch won't trim down!" Dad was panicked.

Uncle Tom immediately realized we forgot to release the lock. By now we had quite a few spectators watching, some laughing out loud. Swishy's theory was now proven on our first launch.

Dad, now with a boat cushion in one hand and a paddle in the other, was trying to manually row his way back to the dock. "Someone throw me a line!" he yelled, with a voice now two octaves higher than when the launch started. In a last desperation maneuver, Dad fired up the motor and threw the throttle forward aiming the bow directly at the dock. With Uncle Carl patiently but anxiously waiting on the dock, Dad had no way to make any fine movements and was again helpless to the wind, which blew him slightly south of the dock and directly into a row of dingys lined up alongside it. A dingy is a small, wooden rowboat used by the commercial fishermen to get from the shore to their boats, which are moored in the harbor. Not only did

Dad slam into many of the fishermen's boats on their moorings, but he also took out nearly all their dingys. The sound of the small dingys cracking from our boat's impact reminded me of the original *Rocky* movie when Stallone is using the slabs of beef as a punching bag. A broken dingy and a broken rib sound alike.

After this thirty-minute fiasco, the boat was finally secured back onto the trailer, and the motor was unlocked. We re-launched without incident now that the crew was reshuffled: Rob behind the wheel and Dad in the passenger seat.

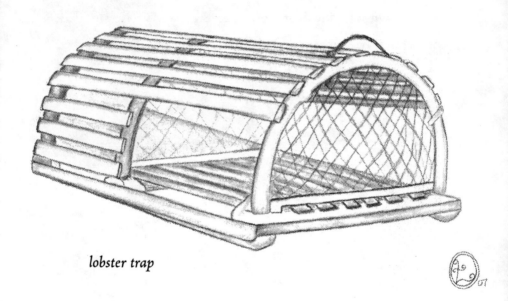

lobster trap

Chapter Four

In The Beginning

The first member of the Seidel family to discover and explore the outer beaches of Cape Cod was my father's younger brother Robert, (a.k.a. Uncle Bob). In the early 1970s, upon the advice of a coworker at General Motors, Uncle Bob and girlfriend Janice set out to vacation on this unknown peninsula. During their first visit, Uncle Bob was quick to realize that this area had much to offer, in fact, much more than he ever expected. With the New Jersey coastline as his standard for comparison, this place had beautiful beaches in a natural and unspoiled setting. The fishing was superb and unpressured. There was no trash, no pollution, and no crowds. The cuisine was simple and fresh. Landscape art, history, antiques, and nautical artifacts were everywhere. Uncle Bob appreciated these things and knew that this area was unique and special. He also knew this would not last forever and wanted to share it with his family.

Uncle Bob could best be characterized as a blend of Curt

Gowdy, John Travolta, Joe Namath, and John Wayne. He expressed a love for the outdoors, conservation, sports, and the old fashioned American way. Add to this an appreciation for wine, deep knowledge of history, and a love for disco and doo-wop music and the package is complete. Unlike my father's bag of black cats, Uncle Bob's bag is very neat and organized, full of cleaning products and utensils, and a few horseshoes and four-leaf clovers. He had so much good luck, that even in times of bad luck, he did well. I can recall one time when Uncle Bob and I were trolling with white buck-tail jigs in the bay for bluefish and bass. He had borrowed an expensive rod from a coworker and placed it, along with my rod, off the back of the boat, propped up at a thirty-degree angle. While we were relaxing under a clear blue sky, Uncle Bob's borrowed rod was suddenly launched off the back of the boat like a rocket. In forty feet of water, the rod was surely unsalvageable. Now angered with the loss of a rod that he did not own, Uncle Bob spouted out a few expletives. Within a couple minutes from the time the rod was launched, I yelled, "Fish on, fish on!"

As I reeled in my line, both Uncle Bob and I looked into the water to see what we had caught. As I retrieved line back onto the reel, we saw a long, thin, white object appear from the depths.

"You caught my rod! You caught my rod!" Uncle Bob screamed as the fishing rod neared his boat.

Miraculously, my buck-tail jig had hooked Uncle Bob's borrowed rod as it was pulled away from our boat. We brought the rod on board and Uncle Bob reeled in his nemesis, a four foot sand shark that stole his rod. Another four-leafed clover blessed his day.

Uncle Bob never married and has no children, but he has treated all of his nieces and nephews as if they were his own children, never missing a birthday party or special event. I spent many fishing and hunting adventures with Uncle Bob and have especially fond memories of our trips to the Adirondack Mountains in upstate New York, where he taught me a lot about nature, trout fishing, and life. After returning from his first week on the Cape, Uncle Bob quickly convinced the rest of our family that this place was worth the trip.

The following year Uncle Bob led the first expedition, which included my grandparents, Nana and Pop Seidel, my parents, and brother Rob and me. We stayed at the Ocean Breeze Cottages. I don't have much recollection from this early time as I wasn't much older than six or seven. I do recall the many stories generated from this time as told by my family through the years. To this day Uncle Bob must be given credit for discovering Cape Cod. When it comes down to it, Uncle Bob was our family's Miles Standish. He also is the only Seidel ever to water-ski on Cape Cod Bay. Additionally, Uncle Bob was the first to hook and land a large striped bass on a rod and reel (Johnson silver minnow to be precise), and held this record for nearly thirty years until his record was broken in 2004 by my sister Kristen, who landed a thirty-five-pound striper on our boat, *The Watermonkey*, off Race Point. He contests this record still today, arguing that his record should stand because Kristen's fish was caught on a rod and reel that she did not own, thus nullifying her place in history.

The Ocean Breeze was a beautiful colony of small, quaint cottages lying directly on the bayside beach along Route 6A, the Cape Cod equivalent of California's Route 1. Ozzie was the owner, a tall, thin gray-headed native Cape Codder who ran a very tight ship. His cottages were immaculate, with gray-painted cedar shakes with white shutters and white flower boxes under the windows; white, pressed sheets and shiny, buffed hardwood floors. Ozzie catered to the older retired folk and quickly took a liking to Nana and Pop. Every evening, the guests gathered on the deck overlooking the bay for cocktails before dinner. Piña coladas, martinis, and imported beer were served while the retired folk shared stories of the adventures they had that day. Whale watch sightings, beach glass finds, and bargains at the flea market were all hot topics of conversation. As the sun set over Provincetown, the wind picked up and the temperature fell, so the older folks donned their jackets and sweaters and quietly headed toward town for their evening meal. My grandparents ate out most nights, usually with friends, and treated the family to dinner twice during the week. One night would involve the whole clan at a large family restaurant like Captain Higgins, the Moors, or the Whitman House. The other night was reserved for only the adults, minus one poor soul who was chosen (or volunteered) to stay behind and baby-sit us children. On this night, the adults wore sport coats and dresses. They were heading to the Christopher Ryder House for dinner, dancing, and a show. A landmark restaurant in Chatham, the Christopher Ryder House was the home of an old sea captain, converted into a dinner theater in the mid fifties. My family, to this day, speaks of the wonderful music and food they enjoyed in this unique establishment. Unfortunately, the restaurant was closed in 1983 and sold as town homes.

Just as quickly as Ozzie became attached to my grandparents, he quickly became detached and disliked their offspring. It soon became apparent that Ozzie and his wife, while very hospitable and affable to old retired folk, held a great distrust and dislike for families with young children. The Ocean Breeze was very happy in its role as the "retirement cottages to the rich old fogies," but did not appreciate any disruptions.

Two young, loud, and boisterous children were not exactly welcomed with open arms to the Ocean Breeze. Neither were Pop's sons, Richard (Dad), and Robert (Uncle Bob). Dad and his brother were fishermen, first and foremost. Unlike most of Ozzie's guests, the thought of quietly lying on the sand baking in the sun just didn't appeal to them. My mother and her sister, Aunt Margie, usually sustained third-degree burns on the first day of vacation, their red, exposed skin later to evolve into severe blisters and intense, burning pain for the remainder of the week.

Mom often spoke of needing to go home with a good tan (a.k.a. burn) as evidence of her travels, "so the girls at work know I've had a vacation." My father often sustained similar damage, only his was accidentally inflicted while pursuing fish in a wide open boat in the bay under an unremitting sun.

I can't recall the words or expression produced by Ozzie when he saw my family pull up in front of his quaint villa in an old broken-down pick-up truck towing an old, faded brown four-teen-foot boat packed to the gills with supplies. I imagine it was something like "Oh shit!" or worse. Needless to say, Ozzie was a gracious host, especially to Nana and Pop Seidel. Dad, always and forever a packrat, promptly unloaded his equipment from the truck and boat, laying most of it along Ozzie's well-manicured cottage. Fishing rods, tackle boxes, eel traps, clam rakes, gaffs, outriggers, filet knives, fishing nets, crab traps, anchors, rope, oil cans, fish finders, oars, boat cushions, rain gear, boots, waders, and spacheling buckets most of which still dirty with seaweed, sand, and fish scales from prior trips. To this day, regardless of the location, Dad always lines up his equipment along the outside of the house as he has done for the past thirty-five years. Organized chaos. If Dad is Oscar Madisen, Ozzie was certainly Felix Unger, and like oil and water, the two didn't mix.

It wasn't that Ozzie disliked fishermen; in fact, his next door neighbor, Old Man North, was a very prominent local fisherman who often ventured out into the black ocean after dark in pursuit of striped bass to bring Ozzie fresh fish the following morning. Actually, it was through Ozzie that we were introduced to Chick, the godfather of the bluefish. However, Ozzie disliked young fisherman, especially those named Richard, with young children, who placed their cluttered gear alongside his cottages.

Most of Ozzie's senior guests headed out to dinner after happy hour and the cottages were quiet for the remainder of the evening. That is until Dad and the Seidel clan come to town. Our family couldn't afford to go out to dinner most nights and, therefore, we stayed back in the cottages and cooked dinner, as many normal people do. Dad always made his famous clam chowder with his secret ingredient—salt pork, which could be smelled from a mile away. We also enjoyed fresh seafood, especially my father. My grandmother had a true love for the taste of lobster and must have genetically passed this trait down to my father, me, and now my daughter Madisen, for we all love lobster more than most other types of food. My grandmother loved a "lazy man's lobster," which is chunked lobster meat served in a crock of melted butter. My father, on the other hand, always goes for the King of the Sea, boiled and not cracked. This has since become the preferred method of preparation for our family's lobsters for the past three generations. That first year, my father purchased an eight-pound lobster, which he stored in Ozzie's cottage refrigerator in anticipation of a seafood feast later that evening.

In the last hours before its execution, that eight-pound

lobster—with claws the size of small footballs—decided to make one last effort to escape and completely destroyed the refrigerator that imprisoned him. The glass shelf was cracked in two and the door was ripped from its hinges; it was clear the lobster did everything in its power to break out. Despite its efforts, the huge lobster was discovered on the shiny, waxed kitchen floor of the cottage and was boiled and eaten that night. Prior to the feast, martinis were served along with homemade clam chowder and fresh, tossed salad. Ozzie and his wife were invited, but gracefully declined. The following day, my father had to break the news to Ozzie that his lobster had destroyed the refrigerator. Ozzie took the news well, never inviting my father back to the Ocean Breeze again.

Pop Seidel was a good storyteller and quite a charismatic fellow. He was a professional drummer and avid sportsman. Pop was introduced to Cape Cod at the same time as my father and me and had a similar passion for fishing. I can recall many days in my father's boat fishing in the bay with Dad, Pop, Uncle Bob, and Uncle Tom, talking about everything while we slowly dragged Rebels and feather jigs behind thick, trolling rods with wire line. The terns dropping into the water after millions of shimmering sand eels swimming under the boat signaled that there were fish nearby. "Fish on!" we yelled and the closest person reached for the rod. Out of respect, the bouncing rod would be handed to Pop, who confidently accepted and battled the fish. Always a bluefish on the end of the line, ranging from twelve to twenty pounds, the battle ensued. Pop, good for about two or three fish, would soon tire, yielding to allow the younger chaps to battle the bluefish. Pop would always be well-protected from the sun with plenty of sun block, large round sunglasses, beige mesh boat shoes, wide-brimmed hat and a towel that he laid over his thighs. Dad always allowed me to fight the next fish, having me on his lap with both arms to secure me. I still remember the power of the fish through the rod, as they strained my seven-year-old arms.

On one occasion, we were trolling in deep water near the large green buoy marker one mile off the tip of the Cape. We weren't seeing any bird activity and as best I recall were probably heading back to the boat ramp. I, about eight years old, was drifting off to sleep on a few boat cushions covered by a beach towel when all of a sudden the reel began to scream. The rod was bent in half and Pop was handed the rod to do battle. This time the opponent was no mere bluefish; it was too strong and too heavy. As Pop took the rod, he was pulled to the side of the boat and at age seventy fell on top of me, awakening me from a semi-conscious state.

"Woop, woop, woop, we got a good one here!" exclaimed Pop is his usual calm manner. He battled the fish for a full forty-five minutes, finally to bring to the boat a large shark, nearly five feet in length. Admittedly, a five-foot shark by today's standards is not very impressive, but consider four adults and a child in a fouteen-foot boat two miles offshore in the middle of Cape Cod Bay with a five-foot shark on one end of the line and a seventy-year-old man on the other, and you might get my point. The shark was hooked on a clear plastic eel rig and was bleeding profusely by the time it reached the boat. Exhausted, semi-comatose, and exsanguinating, the shark sank rapidly like a World War II fighter plane shot down over the South Pacific after the hook was cut from its mouth. A spiral of bright red blood followed the shark as it sank into the depths.

"That fella will be alright," said my grandfather. "He wasn't hooked bad." Even I knew the truth at age eight. That poor shark was dead before he hit the bottom. Pop was hell on sharks.

Pop could also be hell on my dad, who catered to him as a loyal son. We always launched the boat in Provincetown Harbor and headed over to Ozzie's beach to pick up Pop on the days he fished. Pop was a stickler for punctuality and always had to be returned to the beach on time in order to clean up and attend the five o'clock happy hour promptly. I recall one afternoon while heading back to the beach, my father's steering cable snapped, severing our ability to control the direction of the motor from the steering wheel. Knowing he would be late, Pop shouted, "Jesus Christ, Richard! Don't you have anything on this boat that works right?" I think deep down, Dad probably felt like tossing Pop overboard and letting him swim back to shore.

Instead, he graciously said, "Don't worry, Pop, we'll get you back safe." Dad then wrapped both his arms around the top of our old Johnson forty-horse motor and, with a continuous bear hug, guided us back toward the beach. I was promoted on this trip to the rank of first mate for gently controlling the throttle on our way to shore as well as showing more courage and maturity in the face of adversity than my seventy-year-old grandfather. Now safe on dry land, Pop waved us off, anxious to have Dad's boat gone from sight before his friends saw what type of vessel from which he fished.

Speaking of Pop, he was very likable and popular at Ozzie's. Not many of the seniors were fishermen. Pop told many stories of the huge bluefish he took in the bay with his sons. Many of the Ocean Breeze guests asked Pop to show them some of these huge fish so they could see them with their own eyes. One day, Dad, Uncle Bob, Uncle Tom, and I picked Pop up on Ozzie's beach and ventured out for a day's fishing. We returned that afternoon with five beautiful eighteen-pound bluefish, which we lined up parallel on the beach. The senior citizens at Ocean Breeze were amazed at our catch, and Pop became a local hero, bragging of his struggles with the toothy beasts. Dad and the rest of us stood in the background along the boat as Pop took the spotlight. Cameras were snapping as Pop held up his beautiful catch to the amazement of the crowd. Just think, only a year before, we couldn't distinguish a bluefish from a shark and certainly didn't know how to catch one.

scallop shell

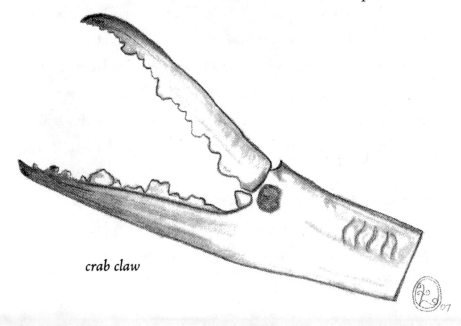

crab claw

Chapter Five

Mary Lou's

After two years at the Ocean Breeze, my parents were notified by Ozzie that they were no longer welcomed back. Citing irreconcilable differences, it was made clear that while Nana and Pop were valued guests, their children and extended family were not. The lobster incident, screaming kids, and the overwhelming amount of fishing paraphernalia all probably contributed. By this time, however, our family had become hooked on Cape Cod for all its beauty and character, and we would continue to return despite our eviction. Well, I should say "non-renewal."

The Little Skipper was another beautiful cottage community about a mile down the road from the Ocean Breeze. Mary Lou, a petite, middle-aged single Portuguese woman native to Truro, owned and managed the property. Mary Lou was extremely pleasant and enjoyed conversation as well as young children. Her cottages were not nearly as well-manicured as Ozzie's, but were clean nonetheless and were mostly occupied by young couples with children. The Little Skipper was buzzing with activity all day, and the only old folks I can recall were my grandparents. Another huge bonus offered by the Little Skipper was that Mary Lou welcomed fishermen. She graciously allowed Dad to park his boat and trailer on her crushed clam-shell parking lot and didn't mind at all when we unloaded all the equipment and lay it alongside her cottage. Mary Lou's Little Skipper would be our Cape Cod summer playground for the next several years. The majority of my most vivid and fondest memories were made during this time, when I was age ten through fourteen.

When Dad pulled into the parking lot tired from his all-night drive, brother Rob and I would erupt from the back of the pickup and run down the wooden walkway and jump off the last plank into the warm sand. Within seconds, we were down by the bay shore collecting hermit crabs and shells in our new shiny plastic buckets. We would have stone-skipping competitions in the water.

The bay water was always warm and clear in August. Many hardshell crabs inhabited the area, and I would love to lure Rob out into the water barefooted and then laugh as his toe was pinched by an angry crab. I'd also sneak up behind him armed with a hermit crab as my living leatherman's tool and allow it to grab hold of the back of Rob's neck or foot. He would immediately cry and scream as if his jugular vein had been severed and run up the beach to the safety of my mother's arms, milking the incident for all it was worth. He knew the more sympathy generated from any of these incidents, the more bounty he might collect in the form of toys or candy when shopping with Mom in Provincetown.

"Ricky, you stop tormenting your brother! Go help your father unload the truck!" I would gladly run back to the cottages to help Dad unload, not because I wanted to, but because I knew I needed to get to him first.

"Ricky, did I hear your brother screaming down by the bay? What happened?"

"Rob stepped on a clam shell, Dad."

"Is he bleeding?"

"Nah, he'll be all right. Mom's got him."

"Ok, then help me untangle the fluke rigs."

Dad always carried at least two spackling cans, which housed his fishing lures. Many fishing lures of all shapes, sizes, and colors were hung by their rear hook from the inner rim of the bucket. At the bottom of the bucket lay soft plastic baits, rust-stained feather jigs, leader, and swivels—all entangled and wet with a mildewed, rusty slime that had been fermenting for years since the last time this chaos was organized. We often found skeletons and mummified carcasses of large black American eels and smaller silver sand eels used for bait the year before. If your bare hands were ever exposed to this tackle, you would carry the putrid scent of rusted metal and rotten fish oil for days.

Meanwhile, I would pray that Rob would stay away long

enough to forget the incident and not spill his guts to Dad, which could potentially mean doom for me. Dad rarely spanked us, but the simple threat he made with his loud, stern voice was enough to rattle your cage and convert you back from the dark side. I actually worried more about Dad punishing me in a much more severe way, which would certainly ruin my vacation. If he threatened to leave me back at the cottages and not take me fishing, he might as well crack open my chest and remove my heart, because by age ten, I knew that I needed to fish when I was on Cape Cod. It was like my life-blood.

Once we unloaded and transported the gear into the cottage, Mom would take over and unpack the luggage and food supplies. The refrigerator would be stocked with the items from the cooler: milk, juice, cheese, and eggs half-broken from the journey. The canned beverages would be stacked in the corner of the small kitchen, Shasta sodas for the kids and Old Milwaukee sixteen ounce cans for Dad, maybe a case of Rolling Rock or Budweiser for special occasions. My parents' white, hardcover Samsonite suitcases would lay open like giant clamshells against the bedroom walls since there was never enough room in the small chest of drawers and closets to accommodate all of our belongings.

While Mom was unpacking, Dad would take Rob and me to Sonny's garage to pick up a block or two of ice for the cooler, and then we'd drive to Nelson's Bait and Tackle to get the fishing report and pick up a copy of the tide charts. Nelson's is now a well-known sporting goods store providing tackle, bait, and advice to outer-beach anglers. I guess it has reached celebrity status, as it's been featured in sportsmen's journals and television shows. After many years, we are now recognized as we enter the bait shop and have earned some respect from the locals. With this familiarity comes some secret fishing information not usually offered to strangers, but not too much. Most of our fishing knowledge has been hard-earned on the water and through trusted friends.

By the time we returned to Mary Lou's, Mom had the cottage organized. The kitchen countertops were covered with bread, cakes, English muffins, cereal, and the variety pack of twelve donuts, chocolate, powdered sugar, plain, and cinnamon. Dad ate the plain donuts, dipping them in the sugar bowl while he drank his coffee. Rob and Mom split the powdered sugar and chocolates, and the cinnamon were all mine. Mom placed the green bananas and tomatoes on the kitchen windowsill to ripen in the August sun. By the end of the week, that same windowsill also housed treasures from the bay, namely shells, beach glass, and crab claws.

At the end of the first day, we were usually exhausted, and everyone retired early. Our first night's dinner typically consisted of lunchmeat or tuna fish sandwiches. We sat in the back room of the cottage that faced the beach, all of the screened windows open to allow the brisk, cool wind to enter off the bay. To this day, I enjoy hearing the high-pitched whistle of the wind at night penetrating through the screen mesh. Dad enjoyed a cocktail as he sat in a recliner listening to the Hyannis jazz station on the radio and read his Atlantic Salmon Journal. Rob and I, now dressed for bed in our matching footie pajamas, jumped and wrestled on the bed until one of us fell off with a loud thump on the hardwood floors, which alerted our parents as to our mischievous activities. Mom entered the room and warned us, "You boys better get to bed before your father comes in here." We usually followed her instructions and never slept quite as soundly as we did that very first night of vacation.

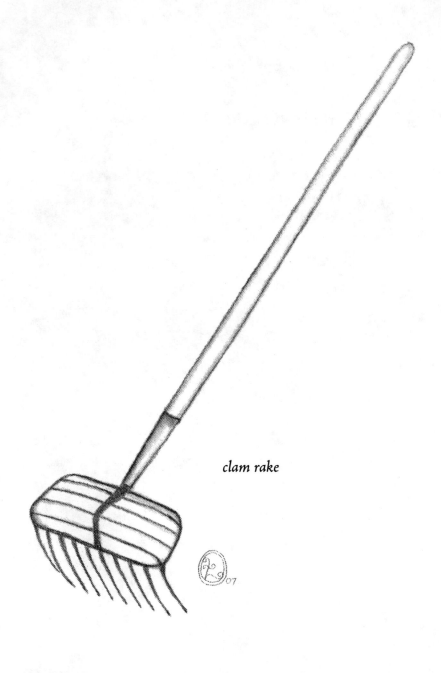

clam rake

Chapter Six

The Squid Incident

The Little Skipper's beach extended for about seventy yards from the deck at the end of Mary Lou's cottages to the edge of Cape Cod Bay. The beach was not as well-manicured as Ozzie's and certainly was not raked or groomed, but was beautiful nonetheless. Many of Mary Lou's guests, including Mom and my Aunts Margie and Carolyn, spent most of the day lying out on the bayside beach. It didn't take my father and Uncle Tom long to discover sea clams and quahogs taking up residence in the bay off of Mary Lou's beach. During low tide they would wade out in water chest high and rake the sand around seaweed beds using four pronged clam rakes. Striking a clam with a rake would sound and feel as if you struck a submerged rock, at which time you would carefully invert the rake, prongs facing up, and gently balance the clam on the rake and bring it to the surface. Sea clams were plentiful and would not only serve as the basic ingredient for my father's famous clam chowder, but would also serve as bait for fluke and flounder fishing. It was not uncommon to impale an unsuspecting hardshell crab with the prongs of the clam rake, which, if mortality wounded, would be dissected on the shore by Rob and me and ultimately devoured by the opportunistic seagulls.

Uncle Neil was the first to experience snorkeling in the bay, and as I grew older, I would do the same. The water in Cape Cod Bay is very clear, and on a calm day the details of its sandy bottom can be seen easily from the surface to approximately twenty feet deep. Until we discovered snorkeling, Rob and I would walk out into the water and collect all sorts of treasures every day of vacation.

Mary Lou's beach was also a place for many land adventures. In fact, this huge sand lot was where Rob and I first learned how to fly a kite. A strong wind in any one direction allowed for an easy launch without even having to taxi down the beach to achieve lift-off. We never had fancy kites, usually just the inexpensive, simple framed-plastic kites designed as a superhero or dragon, tethered by a single string to its midbelly. I never really enjoyed flying kites and thought it quite boring and understood even then why it would be an insult to tell someone to go fly a kite. Rob, on the other hand, enjoyed them, as did Pop Seidel. It was on this very beach where Pop taught us how to send a message up to the kite. Again, I don't understand the reason for this, but Pop patiently instructed us on this process. He wrote a message on a small piece of paper and cut a slit from one edge to the center through which the kite string would be passed. Magically the paper rose up the string all the way to the kite, flying high above as if it were a flag rising up a flagpole. When the paper reached its summit in about ten seconds Pop replied, "Ok, boys, they got our message." Who got our message? Were there aliens up there with whom Pop could communicate? Did Dr. Evil drop Mini Me off on the top of the kite without me knowing? I am a scientist, and I understand that by the laws of physics it is possible to defy gravity and have a piece of paper ascend on a string to a hundred feet in the air. But I still don't know who the hell Pop was sending messages to when it got up there, and I suppose I never will.

As children, Rob and I were always digging holes in the ground. Hoping to dig up a dinosaur bone, Indian arrowhead, new form of life, or buried treasure, we were always excavating something. It didn't take us long to realize that digging in sand was much easier than digging in the hard, anthracite-impregnated dirt of Northeastern Pennsylvania. From our first year at Ozzie's, we enjoyed digging in the sand. As we transitioned to Mary Lou's we became more skilled, and as we grew, our arms were longer each year, and we could penetrate deeper into the sand. Our tools improved as well, and we developed our craft. By ages ten and twelve we now were utilizing metal shovels.

We would build large sand castles and forts, only to run through and destroy them as hurricane Katrina ran through our Southeast last year. I recall one incident when I mistakenly challenged Rob to "bury me alive." Always a mischievous hellion, he gladly accepted the challenge. We were capable of burying each other's limbs, often hip deep in the sand, but rarely deeper since we simply weren't tall enough to reach farther or strong enough to dig through the firmer packed sand. Rob outsmarted me on this occasion. Whether he realized this or not, the deal was made very close the water's edge, where the sand was wet and looser and allowed for deeper excavation. Before long, he had dug a hole that would probably accommodate a fifty-five-gallon oil drum and, as the tide rose, invited me in for a while. Too proud to back down and also curiously excited to face one of my fears head on, I jumped into his grave. Fearing that I would lose my nerve, Rob quickly pushed the damp sand around me to lock me in my tomb. Before long, I was buried up to my neck, paralyzed by the weight of the beach. My mouth and ears were contaminated with the gritty sand, and it took effort to bring air into my lungs for the pressure around my chest. Rob, now exhausted but excited by his achievement, threatened to catch a crab and place it on top of my head. I was reminded of a scene from the movie *Jeremiah Johnson*, where Robert Redford found his mountain man friend buried alive up to his neck by Crow Indians, horse underneath him. In the movie, Redford was able to save his friend from certain death before the Indians returned for his scalp. My fate was more uncertain.

With the tide bringing the water's edge closer to my face by the minute, and Rob searching for a crab, I panicked. Mom was on the beach, but out of earshot. I screamed for help. With each inspiration bringing more sand into my lungs, I was paralyzed and totally helpless. Fortunately, before I lost consciousness from hyperventilation, Pop arrived on the scene and dug me out of this makeshift grave. Covered in a thin layer of sand, I was at last free, and I looked like a plain donut in my father's hand as it was brought out of the sugar bowl. I vowed revenge on my brother as he ran from me to the safety of Mom's beach towel. "Burn you, bubbascubba!" he shouted over and over again.

Another digging skill we mastered as children on Mary Lou's beach was the art of making sand traps. I believe Rob may have been the first kid ever to utilize this method of trapping an unwary beachgoer. A hole eight inches in diameter was dug to about two feet deep. A single paper plate was placed over the top of the hole and the plate then concealed by a thin layer of sand sprinkled on top. My brother yelled, "Hey, slick, come here I found a cool shell." I ran over to meet him, only to fall into his trap. Fortunately for us, children have pliable bones and forgiving joints. While I am not an orthopedist, I do appreciate the potential hyperextension injury that could be induced by falling into my brother's paper plate sand trap. For he, at that time, had no concern for one's medial collateral ligament or anterior cruciate ligament. When the adults were aware of our placing traps, they cautioned us to always fill them back in when we were finished.

"We will, don't worry" was our response. However, one morning my Uncle Neil was carrying his cup of coffee off the deck for a quick barefooted stroll on the beach when his right foot entered one of our traps. Not only did he suffer a sprained right knee, but also second degree burns of his right hand from the coffee. From that day forward, paper plate sand traps were banned from Mary Lou's beach.

My brother is now a highly successful engineer and business executive. Even at a young age, he exhibited entrepreneurial skills by collecting items with plans to resell them for profit, and this was long before Ebay. Our family often talks about one of these business ventures now affectionately referred to as the "squid incident."

The squid is a common cephalopod inhabiting the waters off Cape Cod. Not only served on the dinner table as calamari, it also serves as prey for many gamefish that inhabit these waters. Squid strips are commonly used for fluke bait, while whole squid—in both natural and plastic imitations—are commonly used as bait for bluefish, stripers, and tuna.

One morning when Rob was about ten years old, he discovered hundreds of dead and dying squid lying on Mary Lou's beach at the water's edge. The squid had been chased onto the shore by aggressively feeding bluefish the night before in a falling tide and now were trapped, unable to find their way back into the water. There were many gulls fighting over the carcasses. From prior visits to MacMillan Wharf, my brother knew that squid were caught and sold on the pier every day to fish markets and bait shops. He quickly realized that he had hit the lottery. Hundreds of golden eggs had showered the beach in front of him and were now his for the taking. He knew that there would be jealousy and competition if anyone else knew of his find, so he kept his intentions secret. Shortly after making his discovery, Rob was invited out for a day's fishing with the rest of the family, including me, Dad, and Uncles Neil, Tom, and Bob. However, on this day Rob declined. "Not feeling too good" was his excuse. "I'll just stay behind and help Mom today." Another lie. We all knew that Rob would never volunteer to help Mom unless there was something in it for him.

"Your brother must really be sick, Ricky. First he doesn't want to go fishing, and then offers to help his mother. We better get him to the doctor. Something's really wrong with him."

We all laughed as we pulled away from the cottages. Secretly, Rob knew he would have the last laugh as his pot of gold lay waiting for him at the end of Mary Lou's beach. Now with some of his competition gone for the day, Rob confided in my grandparents and Mom as to his intentions. He assured them that the squid carcasses would be carefully collected in a safe, water-tight bag and be promptly sold later that day. The squid would definitely not be brought into the cottage. I'm sure that the adults involved in this venture thought that Rob would return from the beach with a few squid in a bucket of water to keep and show every-one, only to release them back to the gulls for their extermination. Little did they realize his true intentions.

Rob headed down to the beach, not with pail in hand, but with a black lawn and leaf garbage bag. For the next hour or two he collected every dead squid he could find. With the garbage bag heavy, three-quarters full of squid, he returned from the beach dragging his bounty like a miniature Grinch hauling the Hoos' Christmas back to his lair. Along the way, as the bag was dragged, small perforations occurred under the weight of the squid. Finally arriving back at the cottage, Rob decided to store the bag of squid, now dead for hours, on the west side of the building, where it would bake in the hot August sun for the rest of the afternoon.

Before Rob could profit from his undertaking, the squid car-casses began to decompose. The putrid, oily liquid from their decaying flesh began to seep through the perforations in the black garbage bag that was now serving as a crude fermentation vessel. Before the rest of us returned from fishing, Rob's fortune melted, literally, and now created such a stink throughout the Little Skip-per that even the hard-core fishermen had difficulty stomaching the stench. Few things smell worse than rotten squid. By dusk, other renters began to question the origin of the smell, several of them blaming Fishin' George and his crew. Still, Mom and my grandparents were unaware of Rob's bounty and probably had for-gotten about the business intentions he expressed that morning.

As the pungent smell now permeated into our cottage, Nana had to investigate. She followed her nose to the west side of the cottage where a black garbage bag lay, twisted shut, releasing an oily fluid out of the bottom. Flies swarmed the bag by the dozens. She realized that this was the source of the odor, but did not realize what lay dead within the bag. Mistakenly, she untwisted the bag, releasing a cloud of poison, toxic, nuclear stench, which straightened her curly hair and induced immediate vomiting. She bravely went so far as to spill some of the bag's contents, which were barely identifiable as squid.

"Robert!" she yelled. "Are you responsible for this?"

"Yeah, Nana, I told you I was going to collect squid and sell them on the wharf."

"You didn't tell me you were going to collect a whole school of squid and then use them to poison the entire Cape! Now get these squid back into the water where the gulls can clean them up!"

Rob, realizing what effects the sun can have on dead squid, reluctantly dragged the bag—now reinforced inside a second garbage bag—back to the bay, releasing his prize to the sea. Nana and Mom then applied bleach and other cleaning agents to the west side of the cottage to overcome the smell, and Fishin' George was rightfully vindicated.

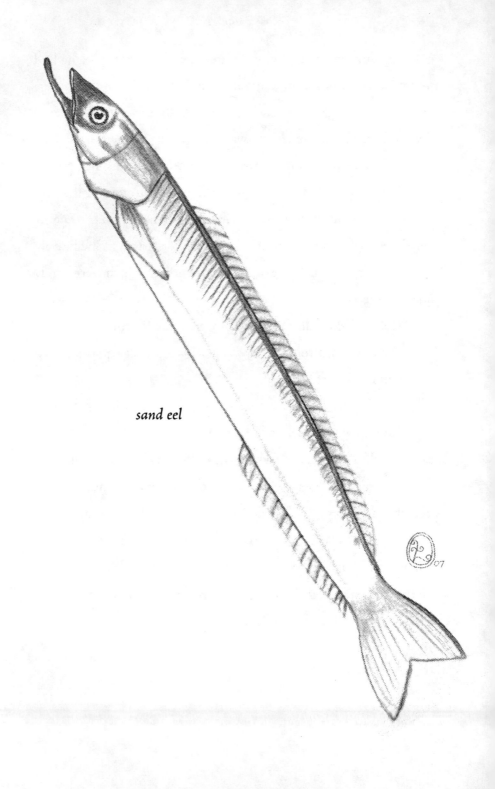

sand eel

Chapter Seven

Fishin' George

Next to family, no one is discussed more than Fishin' George when Cape Cod tales are being told. Our family was first introduced to Fishin' George and his brother-in-law Paulie through Mary Lou at the Little Skipper. George and Paulie were New York City firemen who, along with their wives and children, vacationed at the Little Skipper for years. In fact, when Mary Lou decided to sell her cottages, the two closest to the beach were bought by George. As legend has it, through stories told by Dad and Uncle Bob, Fishin' George was possibly the deadliest striped bass fisherman ever to wet a line off the famous beaches of the Outer Cape.

For several weeks each summer Fishin' George and his clan would rent a small beach house at the Little Skipper. He was a stocky, red-faced man with curly blond hair. Deep fissures scarred his face from years of sun and wind. George always kept a twenty-one-foot center-console Boston Whaler in front of his cottage, but most of his fish were harvested off the beaches. George was a surf fisherman and was motivated not only by a true passion for fishing, but was also equally motivated by the economics of fishing. Throughout the 1970s and early 1980s, striped bass were abundant in the waters off Cape Cod. Their fishery was relatively unregulated, and no limits were placed on the catch. Therefore, a talented fisherman spending his entire vacation focused on harvesting striped bass could do well, pay for the vacation, and earn some extra cash doing what he loves to do. An enabling wife who allowed her husband to fish off the beach all night to return in the morning, clean and sell his catch, and sleep the rest of the day completed the package.

Although I was too young to spend time and learn from Fishin' George, my father and uncles were not. They spent late afternoons watching him prepare his rods for the evening's pursuit. Nine and ten-foot surf rods with huge open-faced reels lined up like columns in two-inch pvc pipe on the front bumper of his white four-wheel drive pickup truck. Extending off both front and rear bumpers, two large ice chests would keep his catch. More long surf rods held in parallel on roof racks extended nearly to the rods in front. He rigged each rod and reel with heavy monofilament line tipped with stainless steel leader. A variety of colorful wooden lures decorated the rods as they attached line to reel: Needlefish, Bottle Plugs, Surface Dannys, Darters, Polaris Poppers, and Creek Chubs of all sizes and colors. Some of his rods were dressed with bare hooks to hold sand eels on the ocean bottom with three and four-ounce triangular lead weights. Finally, perhaps most deadly were his rods baited with a live American eel, a long black slippery snake-like creature fastened to a hook and allowed to swim in the current off the beach and attract hungry fish. As Fishin' George loaded his gear he often shared some of his bass fishing secrets with my father, who traded back some Atlantic Salmon fishing anecdotes. We posed no threat to George at that stage in our striper development. We certainly had the desire and were learning the trade, but we had no means to get to where George was going, the beaches of the Outer Cape. To this day, the only way to reach the fabled waters where rip currents continuously churn baitfish to hungry predators is either across sand or sea. At that time we had no boat capable of reliably getting us to the deep, dark waters off the back side of the Cape at night in unpredictable weather. Getting to the beaches by land required special four-wheel drive vehicles with tires deflated to about 10lb psi and containing special survival equipment. A seasonal permit was required. None of this we had or were capable of obtaining at that time.

As the sun began to lie down on the North Atlantic horizon, George and Paulie would set out over the sand pursuing what they loved to do: catch bass and make money. Several rods, baited with live eel, smaller sand eels, and chunked herring were held up in the sand by spiked pvc pipe and watched over by George and Paulie's kids as they sat near a campfire on the beach. Surf-fishermen, who now littered the beach, waded out into the cold water and tried to maintain their balance against pounding waves and strong undertow. During the falling tide, especially with a full moon, stripers could be heard chasing baitfish to the surface as the men casted their plugs to induce a strike. All along the beaches of the Outer Cape—from Provincetown to Chatham—men would be casting. The fishermen also became organized, communicating via CB radios to inform others as to the locations of fish. These were the days before conservation and catch-and-release.

Each morning as brother Rob and I finished our cereal, Mom getting ready for another day on the beach, and Dad reading over the tide charts, Fishin' George and Paulie would pull up in their pick-up, tires nearly flattened, just off the beach. George's kids would pile out of the back of the truck, still wearing clothes from the day before, hair messed, and smelling of fish. George and Paulie, tired from a full night's work, donned bright yellow raingear over chest-high waders and Woolrich coats. Both coolers on either end of the truck were usually heavy with fresh fish, so many that striper heads and tails kept the lid from shutting all the way.

Fishin' George never spoke much, usually busily working on his gear. One early morning, I walked out of our cottage to see what George had brought in from the night before. Looking up at their rods lined up in pvc pipe along the front bumper of their truck, I spotted a fruit bat impaled on one of the monofilament fishing lines, about two-thirds up the rod. This unfortunate creature must have accidentally flown directly into Fishin' George's rod and split its cranium in two, now stuck to the line. So much for echolocation. Its wings were partially extended, now in rigor mortis, twisting its furry brown body on the line, back and forth, as the wind blew. As I looked closer at its pitiful face, with sharp needle-like teeth showing, the expression on its face said, "What the f…?!" The poor sucker never knew what hit him.

"Mr. Fishin' George, there's a dead bat stuck on your fishing pole. Must have flown into it by accident," I said.

"That's no accident son, it's a new lure I'm trying out," he joked.

"Catch anything on it?"

"Not yet, that's why it's still there." He smiled and went back to work as I scampered back to the cottage to tell Dad of my newly discovered lure.

I can recall many mornings when Mary Lou's wooden sidewalk was covered with striped bass stacked side-by-side, as Fishin' George used a garden hose to wash the sand from their flesh before taking them to the wharf for sale. Thirty to forty stripers, stacked side by side, ranging in size from ten to fifty pounds, every morning for several weeks, every summer for over a decade. It's not hard to understand why the striped bass stock was almost depleted by the mid 1980s, leading to a moratorium on bass fishing for nearly a decade.

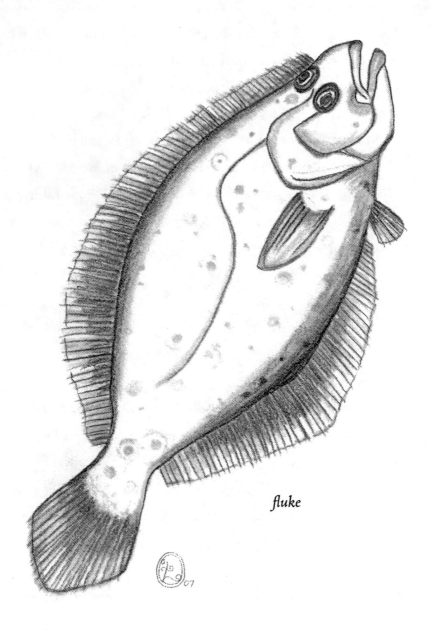

fluke

Chapter Eight

Anyone Seen Uncle Neil?

In the summer of 1979, our family once again stayed at Mary Lou's Little Skipper. The entire extended family was there, inhabiting six of the ten cottages. This was a week that we would have liked to trade back, a week of a nor'easterner. A nor'easterner can be thought of as a weather pattern whereby there is a hovering counter-clockwise airflow continually recycling wet weather off the ocean back to the land mass. This is usually associated with steady rain, wind, high seas, and cool weather. A Doppler weather map would show a lot of cloud cover with a churning counter-clockwise spiral of clouds lying stationary over a certain area for a prolonged period of time. The bottom line is that although we have experienced nor'easterners many times on vacation—some of which lasted for the entire week—it is definitely something you do not welcome. That is, unless you are confined to a wheelchair, blind, and highly allergic to sunlight.

In any event, most vacations plagued by nor'easterners

are spent indoors, sharing stories inside the cottage, touring museums, shopping, and fighting off depression. My father would always advocate getting out of the cottage during these times in an effort not to become more depressed and fall into what he phrased a "slough of despond." Where that term came from I haven't a clue, but it was used often in my childhood to describe what the psychiatry manuals would term "Major Depression." Mom was sometimes predisposed to the slough so it was important to practice preventative medicine and get her out of the cottage, even in the most foul weather. Mom would enjoy perusing the gift shops and stores that line Commercial Street in Provincetown. Her favorite stop was Cabot's Fudge Shop, an old white two-story structure that sits on a corner across from Town Hall. Through the large front window, you can observe an antique saltwater taffy machine as it transforms an amorphous sticky glob of sugar into a long tubular rope, then guillotining it into small chunks, wrapping them with waxed paper, twisting each side, and dropping them into a large storage basket. All the colors and flavors of the rainbow are produced in this manner. Solid colors, swirled multi-colors, and everything in-between. The smell of the fresh candy and fudge is overwhelming as you pass through the front door. All varieties of fudge are kept behind large glass-paneled counters with plenty of sample pieces to be tried. Mom is what you would consider a "frequent flyer" at the fudge shop, analogous to Norm on the sitcom *Cheers*. When she passes through the front door of Cabot's, the owner sitting at the cash register and some of the long-time employees behind the counters always yell out "LaVerrrrrrrrrrnnnnnnnnnnnnne!"

Strolling through candy stores and fudge shops with Mom was fine for Rob and me when we were youngsters and still is enjoyed by my sisters to this day. However, as Rob and I grew older, we needed to spend wet, cold, rainy days doing manly things with Dad. Dad was also an eternal optimist. In the darkest, stormiest weather, even when the meteorologists were predicting rain throughout the week, Dad would always propose a better forecast. I suppose when you bust your ass all year to earn enough money to take your family on vacation, the last thing you want to do is let bad weather get you down. As we drove down Route 6 toward one of Dad's favorite haunts—namely bait and tackle shops, such as the Goose Hummock Shop, Black Duck Sporting Goods, Nelson's Bait and Tackle, or Lands End Hardware Store—with the sky full of gray clouds and the rain falling at a forty-five-degree angle to the Earth from strong gusty winds, Dad was not dissuaded. With the truck's windshield washers at maximum pace, he would often point way off in the distance and say, "See that over there guys, it's starting to lighten up. I think I see the sun trying to break through the clouds. This will probably burn off soon and we may be able to launch this afternoon. What time is high tide?"

This prediction would revive us from our slough like a large bolus of Prozac. We could now enjoy our visit to the tackle shop as Dad would pick out some "deadly" lures to be used on big fish that week. Just as colorful as the saltwater taffy bins at Cabot's were the rows and rows of saltwater lures. All shapes and sizes of lures made from hard and soft material—wood, plastic, stainless steel, lead, feathers, and fur—hung from racks throughout the stores. Most of the time Dad's weather predictions were unsubstantiated and wrong, but occasionally his hopeful forecasts proved to be true. Whether this was a mere freak of nature or divine intervention, I can recall days when the sun did break through the clouds, a warm mist rising off the blacktop road as we drove back from the tackle shop. A beautiful rainbow connected the Heavens to the bay. We would fish that day. All was right in the world.

As the week progressed without signs of a weather break, sometimes we became desperate and took risks in order to get out in the boat and fish. One such occasion was that summer of 1979. The men were about to go stir-crazy now, waking on day five of their one-week vacation to hear that all-too-familiar sound: the monotonous ping of raindrops striking the ground outside. On this morning it appeared that the wind was diminishing, and there were few whitecaps on the bay. Uncle Bob offered to launch his boat that morning and looked for volunteer shipmates. I was quick to step forward, hoping that Mom would allow me to go. For some reason, my father did not elect to go out that day, maybe he had a premonition, or maybe he was now victim to the slough of despond. Uncles Tom and Neil also volunteered for the journey and promised to take good care of me. We loaded the gear. Frozen sea clams were taken from the ice box for bait, and we headed to the boat launch. Prior to our departure a treaty was struck with the women who demanded that we would only fish in the harbor, which was well-protected from severe weather, and would immediately return if the seas became worse or lightning appeared. We would by no means take any chances, especially with a twelve-year-old on board.

As we arrived at the boat launch in Provincetown, the wind began to pick up and blew into our direction bringing larger waves with it. As my uncles trepidatiously stared out over the harbor I knew exactly what they were thinking and promised myself that I would not act disappointed when the trip was cancelled. Uncle Bob scratched his head and turned to Uncle Tom.

"Tommy, you think we've got enough beer in the cooler?" asked Uncle Bob.

"It wouldn't hurt to get another twelve-pack. I'll run over to the package store while you guys get the boat ready. I think I'll pick up some blood worms as well," said Uncle Tom.

Yes! My fears were resolved. The trip was not cancelled after all! We loaded our gear, coolers, and bait and awaited Uncle Tom's return.

I was placed in the boat while it was still on the trailer, and it was slowly backed down the boat ramp. Uncles Neil and Tom stood knee deep in the cold water watching as the rear axle became submersed.

"Whoa!" shouted Uncle Neil. "Far enough."

The boat was unlatched and pushed off the trailer. Uncle Bob pulled forward and parked the boat and trailer in the empty parking lot. I noticed that my uncles were having some difficulty stabilizing the boat in the water as the incoming waves relentlessly pounded them, forcing water half-way up their backs.

"Let's go boys!" shouted Uncle Bob as the motor was lowered, and the boat was turned into the oncoming waves. A steady, salty mist fell and covered us as if we had just gotten out of a cold, saltwater sauna. The waves were enlarging as we left the boat ramp. Looking back to a parking lot that is almost always full, and seeing my Uncle Bob's truck and trailer as the sole occupants, I began to question our judgment.

I asked my uncles if they thought we should turn back because it seemed a lot rougher than we anticipated. Uncle Neil shared my concerns, now wearing a hooded rubber raincoat, his wet, curly brown hair falling from his forehead onto his glasses, now completely opacified by the rain and salt mist. The ruling was made by Captain Bob, who was now directing the boat perpendicular to the shore, angling the boat to reduce the impact of the crashing three to four foot waves. Despite this, the waves continued to crash over the side and windshield of the boat, sometimes bringing enough water to float the cooler and tackle boxes. We were now all soaking wet and had only left the boat ramp five minutes ago. Uncle Bob knew that we were heading for safer waters. The harbor is surrounded hemicircumferentially by a horseshoe-shaped landmass and breakwater. If we could reach the inner portion of the harbor adjacent to the breakwater, the water there would be calm.

"It'll get worse before it gets better boys," shouted Uncle Bob as he gritted his teeth on the filter of his cigarette, now extinguished by the rain and waves.

Finally, as we approached the land mass on the harbor opposite the boat ramp, things got better. The wind was now buffered by the peninsula of dunes separating the harbor from the ocean and the seas calmed. We had finally reached our destination, cold and wet, but still afloat and eager to start fishing. We dropped the anchor and allowed the boat to drift several yards before the anchor bit into the sandy bottom and the rope became taut. We were fishing for fluke and flounder in an area well-known for both species. These fish are close cousins distinguished from each other by several characteristics. Fluke are larger and have a hinged jaw and sharp teeth, while flounder are toothless and have jaws more like a bluegill. Both species are flat, with a white underbelly and mottled brown back, having both eyes on top of their head. My hook was baited with pieces of clam belly and tossed over the starboard side of the boat.

"Why don't you try a blood worm, Ricky?" asked Uncle Tom

as he handed me the flat, brown box containing dozens of these slimy creatures entangled in clumps of seaweed. He knew exactly why I elected to use the clams. Any child in their right state of mind would fear the blood worm as I did. The blood worm is a creature harvested from the shallow, sandy bottoms of the bay and used to catch flounder, who consider them a delicacy. They look like a cross between a nightcrawler and a centipede, but contain a secret weapon. Retracted into their head lie two needle-like curved prongs similar to the clippers on the head of a hellgrammite. If the blood worm is disturbed and manipulated by inexperienced hands, it will unmask its hidden weapons and launch them forcefully into the handler's flesh, immediately inducing a painful sting. Therefore, I graciously refused my uncle's offer.

It wasn't long before we started catching fluke, sometimes two fisherman doing battle at once. These fish were fair-sized, most over the legal limit of fifteen inches. We kept some of the larger fish to present to Nana that evening. Uncle Bob boated his first sea robin of the trip and asked Uncle Tom to release it for him. The sea robin is a bottom-feeding scavenger fish that is not fit for human consumption. It is frequently caught when fishing for other bottom fish and serves no other purpose than pure nuisance. Looking like a cross between bird, fish, and lobster, it has several spiny legs protruding from its underbelly and rounded wing-like pectoral fins.

"Release your own damn sea robin, Robert, that thing is too ugly for me to get near," replied Uncle Tom.

Just after uttering those words, Uncle Tom's rod was nearly ripped from his hands. The hook was set, and he began to do battle with a large fish. We knew immediately that the beast on the end of his line was a worthy adversary and not typical of the fluke we had been catching. Respectfully, we all reeled up our lines to allow more unimpeded room for the battle.

Uncle Tom struggled for nearly twenty minutes with this creature, initially caught on the bottom twenty feet away, but quickly stripping nearly a hundred yards of his twelve-pound test line. His rod now bent nearly 360 degrees.

"Don't horse 'em in, Tommy, whatever you do! You're into a monster down there!" screamed Uncle Bob.

"Nah, he's hooked up with a lobster pot or anchor down there, maybe an old boot," Uncle Neil replied sarcastically.

We all knew this was not true as we were stationary at anchor and whatever was at the end of Uncle Tom's line was moving for its life, now appearing to weaken. Tom started gaining some ground on the beast and was able to retrieve some line. The line whistled from the wind as beads of water dripped from the tip of the rod as it bowed straight down into the water. The fish took Uncle Tom to the stern near the motor as he stumbled to keep his balance in the rocking boat. We all stared into the depths following his line in order to get a glimpse of the beast. Finally, a dark shadow appeared as the fish began to surface. It was a huge doormat!

Large fluke are referred to as doormats, because they look just like that. This was the largest doormat that our family has seen to this day. It probably measured at least thiry-two inches in length and was nearly that wide. We watched in awe as Uncle Tom tried to bring the fish closer to the boat.

"Don't lose him, Tommy! Keep him out of the motor!" shouted Uncle Bob as he realized the implications of such a catch. Up to this point, Uncle Bob held our family's record for the largest striper caught on the Cape, and now would also claim the largest fluke, a title he would share with Uncle Tom, who actually hooked and battled the fish.

However, as the monster neared the net, which was likely not large enough to contain the fish, as quickly as it took the bait, the line snapped. Uncle Tom fell back into the boat, and all was lost. Uncle Bob yelled out, "Tommy, what the hell did you do? I told you not to horse that fish," obviously disappointed that his record was now swimming back to the bottom of the bay.

"One more word out of you and you'll be swimming back to shore!" Uncle Tom barked back in an exhausted and frustrated tone of voice.

As we reflected on what happened over the preceding thirty minutes, we came to realize that what Uncle Tom lost was not likely a fluke but a small Atlantic Halibut, which are sometimes caught in these waters. This made his catch all that much more interesting and exciting, but also that much more disappointing.

By now the skies began to darken, and the rain picked up. The wind direction changed and now blew out to sea away from the boat ramp. We decided to head home for the day. Uncle Tom pulled up the anchor, and the rods were put in the front of the boat. We tossed the remnants of the clams and bloodworms overboard and the last beers were drunk.

"Tommy, check my gas line. Make sure we're connected!" shouted Uncle Bob as the motor failed to fire up.

"We're connected," Uncle Tom pumped more gas into the line.

"She's not turning over, what's wrong Robert?" asked Uncle Neil.

"I don't know, either the motor's flooded, or we have a carburetor problem. Either way we'll need a tow. Tommy drop that anchor again so we don't get blown out to Spain."

I thought back to our launch four hours ago and realized the implications of an empty boat-launch parking lot. Plenty of parking and no competition for fishing spots, but also no one around to provide a tow in the event of an emergency. In 1979, before the internet and the era of technological marvels, we were, on one hand, blessed by the solitude of fishing in a boat with no one around, no one capable of bothering us with cell phone or two-way radio. But now we were also cursed by lack of the same technology.

Uncle Bob's boat was compliant with the Coast Guard regulations regarding safety equipment on board. We had the proper number of life jackets, anchor, fire extinguisher, and whistle, but I'm not sure all were in proper working order. By now, dusk was approaching as we sat in the boat, rain falling, hoping against hope that another foolish boater was somewhere on the bay, returning to the harbor boat ramp.

Back at the cottages, the rest of the family began to question our whereabouts. Before long, Nana would call the Coast Guard and report us missing at sea, although we had not been gone long enough for them to launch a formal search. From the Coast Guard standpoint, they had not received any distress signals from that area.

Back in Uncle Bob's boat, there was now some distress. Uncle Neil was the first to openly question our decision to launch that day, as a lobsterman's boat became visible on the horizon heading our way. He reached into Uncle Bob's tool box and grabbed the large stainless steel whistle that sat in the top tray. Waiting until the lobsterman was within earshot, Uncle Neil began to blow on the whistle with all his breath. His cheeks protruded like Louis Armstrong as he trumpeted "When the Saints Go Marchin' In." Uncle Neil, despite his efforts, could not produce a sound. He blew again, even harder this time. Nothing. He shook the whistle and realized that there was no ball inside to produce sound. "God dammit Robert! Don't you have anything that works on this boat of yours?!"

"We're lucky he remembered to put gas in the tanks, let alone check to make sure his whistle works," replied Uncle Tom.

Not able to produce a distress sound, Uncle Neil decided to produce a distress signal as the losterman drew closer. He grabbed two red boat cushions, one in each hand, and began jumping up and down in the boat, as he waved the cushions in the air. "HELP! HELP!" he shouted yelling toward the lobsterman.

"Neil, why don't you take those boat cushions and swim over to that lobsterman's boat, you might get there faster," laughed Uncle Bob as he lit a cigarette and handed Tommy a beer.

"You'll thank me for this later, Robert. I'm the one gonna save your ass!" Just then, the lobsterman turned toward our boat and pulled up alongside.

"You guys need a tow?" he asked.

"You bet. Can you get us to the boat launch? I'll throw you a line."

With a line secured from our bow-hook to the stern of the lobster boat, we were slowly pulled to safety at the boat ramp.

Neil and Tom held the boat stable in the water while Uncle Bob backed the trailer down the boat launch. I stayed inside the boat, gathering our equipment, collecting the empty cans in a garbage bag, and cleaning the opaque windshield with Windex solution.

With the boat now secure, Uncle Bob and Tom decided to haul the boat to the local marina to have it evaluated and repaired while Uncle Neil and I would call for a ride back to the cottages. Neil and I walked down the street to the nearest payphone booth and called his cottage. Everyone was happy to hear that we were still alive, and also angry that we had foolishly ventured out in such weather. Aunt Melinda and Nana agreed to drive to the boat launch and pick us up while Aunt Carolyn prepared an Italian dinner. My father was anxious to hear the fishing report.

Uncle Neil and I stood on the corner near the boat ramp awaiting our ride home. We were both beaten down by the weather, both tired and hungry. I was wearing a baseball cap, saturated pair of denim jeans, and blue sweatshirt covered by a garbage bag with holes cut to allow my arms to protrude. Uncle Neil stood beside me, shoeless with a yellow bathing suit dripping wet and sand coating his lower extremities from mid-calf to foot. He wore a brown, hooded raincoat with raindrops falling from the ridge of his hood, appearing as a horseless ringwraithe from a J.R.R. Tolkien novel.

"Here they are, finally." Uncle Neil saw Melinda and Nana approaching.

Their Buick Monte Carlo drove right by us as if we were not even standing there and turned right at the next corner.

"I'm sure that was them. They must have missed us."

The brown Monte Carlo passed again and again three more times before it finally turned into the boat launch parking lot. Neil and I scampered to the parking lot in order to catch up with the car. When we arrived, Uncle Neil knocked at the window. "Melinda, it's me! Your husband, Neil!"

Melinda and Nana both appeared as if they were looking at strangers. Finally after nearly three minutes of dumbfoundedness, Nana uttered, "Neil, Ricky, is that you?"

"Yes!"

"Are you sure?"

After some further analysis they finally determined that the two people standing before them, appearing as stowaways from the gallows of a fishing vessel, were really their kin and decided to admit us into their car.

Finally, back at the cottage after a hot bath and warm, dry clothes, we shared stories from the day. Uncle Tom was the hero having lost a huge doormat, while Uncle Bob took the heat for leading the expedition into unsafe waters with a child on board. I emerged relatively unscathed and Uncle Neil, to this day, cannot imagine how he could not be recognized by the two most important people in his life: his wife and mother.

seagull

Chapter Nine

An Unfriendly Place

Near the tip of the Cape Cod peninsula stands the Wood End lighthouse, which is perched on a sand dune rising thirty-nine feet into the air. It was constructed in 1872, made of brick with a concrete foundation. Long Point is a beautiful beach along the Atlantic Ocean side of Wood End extending to the Long Point lighthouse at tip of the Cape. Settled in 1818, about 200 people lived on this narrow peninsula during the fishing industry's height in 1850. At that time, it had a school-house with sixty students and a sea salt industry. Henry Thoreau commented on how plentiful the lobsters were in this area, sold to the New York fish markets for two cents a piece. Now uninhabited by man, this area is relatively inaccessible to routine beachgoers in that there is no nearby parking lot or access road. The area is only approachable by way of a vigorous hike across the long granite-block wall known as the breakwater, by private boat, or by the harbor shuttle. Therefore, it is not heavily populated even during the peak tourist season. It is an estuary for gulls and terns, many of which nest along this desolate beach. The ocean around the beach here is clear and drops off quickly to deep depths within a few yards from the water's edge. Offshore there is a large, green buoy heard easily from the beach as it rocks back and forth with the waves, clanging its large bell as it guides tall ships, whale-watching boats, and the Provincetown fishing fleet around the tip of the Cape, and brings them safely into the calm waters of Provincetown Harbor. This same green bell buoy was the site of Pop's shark conquest mentioned in a previous chapter.

Because this area is so beautiful, so desolate, and so inacces- sible, it tends to attract people not wanting to interact with or be pursued by others. These people appreciate beautiful things and like the area for its isolation. The majority of those people inhabiting this area are—you guessed it—gay and lesbian nude sunbathers. We commonly interact with these types of beach-goers in Provincetown and frequently share shuttle rides with them as we take the water taxi to our boat moored in the harbor, while they are taken onward to Long Point for a day's relaxation in the sun wearing nothing more than a gold chain and ankle bracelet. They wear clothes on the shuttle, at least a Speedo and a pair of Birkenstocks.

I can recall many boat trips around Long Point on *The Watermonkey*, trolling just offshore in deep water, looking back at the beach among the dunes, and seeing many young men proudly standing toward the water displaying all that God had given them. Standing tall, hands on their hips as if to say "Here I am, look at me!" Yet, they were on a desolate beach with few people around. As a child, I asked myself: why did they act as if they want people to notice them? The veteran sunbathers could easily be differentiated from the rookies by their tan lines. How long did it take one to develop a confluent tan in that area? Did one use special tanning solutions? What kind of havoc did a severe sunburn in that region create? Did it affect performance? Many questions but no answers.

As we passed by the Long Point beaches, half embarrassed but still curiously looking back toward the beach, Uncle Bob often spouted out, "Where's my slingshot, he's showing me a big target!" Less often, but not infrequently, we passed by nude lesbians on the beach, who often provoked comments like, "Calm down Rich, you're going to give yourself a heart attack!" as my father fogged up his binoculars, after handing over the steering wheel to one of us kids who were disinterested in the activities on the beach. Even less often, we passed a nude sunbather lying across the deck of another vessel in the water. This person would more likely be an attractive heterosexual woman wearing a bikini bottom and no top. Whenever Dad and a few uncles were on board, we immediately slowed down to a drift and threw some fishing lines in the water. My father would glass the area in the direction of the nude boater looking for "bird activity." At that young age, I never knew what attracted fish to the area around nude sunbathers. Now I realize that she was attracting fishermen, not fish. Once the sunbather realized that she was the focus of several horny fishermen, the shirt went back on, fishing rods were brought back into the boat, and we headed out to the fishing grounds.

While my father, brother, and most uncles never personally stepped foot on these beaches, only visiting them as a transient from the deck of our boat, Uncles Carl and Neil actually spent time there, and just like a visitor to Skull Island, nearly came face to face with disaster.

Many years ago, Uncle Neil, after recovering from his knee injury suffered during Rob's sand-trapping period, decided to spend a relaxing, romantic day on Long Point beach with his young bride, Aunt Melinda. Uncle Bob graciously agreed to provide shuttle service with his own boat to and from the beach. With picnic basket packed with fresh French bread, various cheeses, grapes, and a bottle of Gallo's finest sauvignon blanc, Neil and Melinda disembarked from Uncle Bob's Glasstron as he and Pop Seidel sped away in pursuit of large bluefish.

As I said earlier, although the most noticeable inhabitants of Long Point Beach are the nude gay and lesbian sunbathers, the most prevalent inhabitants are the ravenous sea gulls. The beach blanket was gently laid on the sand with shoes placed on the corners to keep the wind from folding it over. The beach umbrella was spiked into the sand and angled to block the direct sun's rays. The portable radio was tuned into the Hyannis jazz station where Cole Porter was serenading the happy couple. All was right in the world.

They poured the wine and broke the bread. A gentle breeze lifted the brim of Aunt Melinda's large floppy straw hat as she applied sunscreen to Neil's back. Within minutes, dark shadows from patrolling gulls began to appear across the sand and blanket. Initially, only a few, but soon dozens of hungry sea gulls were gliding closer and closer to the picnic lunch. With each pass the gulls became more aggressive and mocked my aunt and uncle, squawking as they hovered overhead. Neil's initial strategy was to appease them by offering some of his bread. However, the gulls were unappreciative and were not willing to negotiate or accept anything less than total victory. They soon were whipped up into a blabbering, swarming feeding frenzy not unlike a school of sharks tearing apart a whale carcass. A ground assault was launched from the flank as brave gulls walked directly onto their clean blanket and stole more morsels of food. As they walked off, they dropped bombs from their bottoms, both on land and from the air, riddling the clean beach blanket with splatters of white gull dung. Without any respect for human dignity and in brazen defiance of the Geneva Convention, the gulls began to bomb my brave aunt and uncle as well. On a desolate beach, now themselves splattered with evidence of the attack, Neil and

Melinda huddled close together under the beach umbrella, itself covered in excrement, praying for reinforcements or rescue.

As the battle came to a close, when all the lunch had been devoured by the evil gull Luftwaffe, Neil and Melinda were physically and emotionally scarred. As Uncle Bob and Pop brought the boat into the shallows to pick them up, they clearly noticed something was wrong.

"What's happened to you guys? It looks like you've been through hell!" said Pop.

"We have," muttered Uncle Neil. "We have. Goodbye forever, Long Point Beach."

Other than Uncle Neil and Aunt Melinda, the only other blood relative I know to have visited this area on foot was Uncle Carl. Standing six foot seven inches tall and weighing about 280 in his prime, Uncle Carl was a very daunting man. His appearance by no means represented his demeanor as he to this day remains a very kind, humble, and soft-spoken man. He is always willing to help anyone in any way he can. Unlike most of my uncles, he is not a fisherman. He enjoys boating, but would rather spend his time exploring the natural beauty of Cape Cod on land, particularly old Pilgrim cemeteries. A skilled photographer, he is never without his camera bag, which is filled with professional, quality equipment including various high-powered zoom lenses. An avid walker, Uncle Carl remains the only member of our family to this day to hike out to Long Point Beach over land, which includes a mile walk over the rocky breakwater. The breakwater was constructed in 1911 by the Army Corp of Engineers to prevent large quantities of sand from washing into the harbor. It now serves as home to various fish, crab, starfish, and plant species in the harbor and was a favorite snorkeling destination for my friends and me to explore in high school.

On his day trip to Long Point, he was impressed by the natural beauty of the moors, marshy fields of tidal waters behind the breakwater and the old Long Point Lighthouse with Provincetown as its backdrop. He took many photographs on his journey to the point. Wearing cut-off denim shorts, black socks, white tennis shoes, shirtless, with suspenders over his shoulders, and a red, white, and blue sweatband wrapped around his forehead, Uncle Carl stumbled across the other group of beach inhabitants: topless lesbian sunbathers. Not only were these women surprised by my uncle's tall presence, they were also angered by his mere being there. Always willing to converse with anyone he met, Uncle Carl introduced himself to the group and asked if they visit here often. He even offered to take their portrait and get them copies later in the week when the film was developed. As he reached into his camera bag and pulled out his Nikon F5 35mm camera, donning a high powered zoom/wide-angle lens, the ladies had all they could take.

"Listen you pervert, why don't you take your camera, and yourself, and get your ass off this beach before I take that camera and shove it up there myself!" yelled a heavy-set, topless woman with short, spiked hair, long rat-tail extending down the middle of her back, with at least eight earrings outlining the periphery of her left ear.

Uncle Carl was obviously set aback by this comment. "Why don't you put your tops back on so I can get a more respectable shot, and I won't risk cracking my camera lens?"

With that comment taken as a direct insult and act of war, the group of lesbians quickly surrounded my uncle and began to move in for the kill. Realizing his minutes were numbered and only chance of survival was to retreat, he quickly headed back to the breakwater and scampered back to safety, never to return to Long Point again.

To this day, as we navigate past Long Point beach and the Wood End Lighthouse on our way to the fishing grounds, I still enjoy the beautiful landscape, but remain fearful of this place, tread lightly through these waters, and hope to never lose engine power and become shipwrecked off these shores.

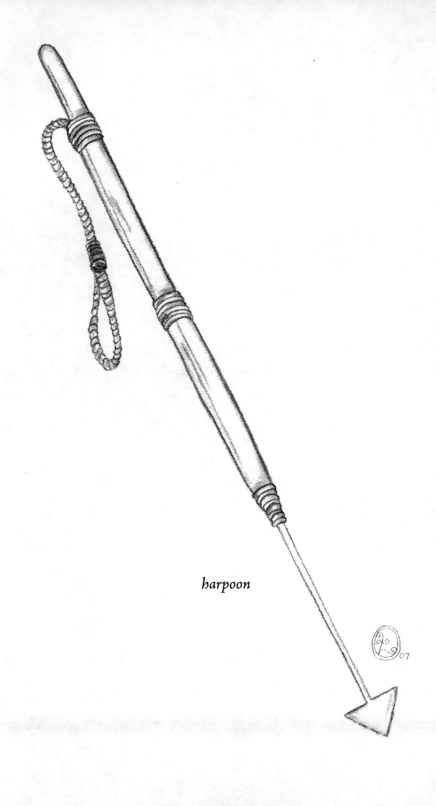

harpoon

Chapter Ten

Water Monkeys

According to the Chinese horoscope, water monkeys are curious and fun-loving creatures. They enjoy a good time with friends and family and love to play practical jokes. Although they have strong intellect, creativity, and intuition, they can often become easily distracted or confused. They can generally accomplish any given task and appreciate difficult and challenging work.

These, however, were not the water monkeys of my childhood as told through the eyes of my father who to this day claims to have first-hand experience with these creatures. In his description, water monkeys are evil creatures who emerge from the depths of the ocean at night in search of bad children.

The water monkey legend was initially told to my father by Charlie Huffman, a one-armed, tobacco-chewing, cigar-smoking, whiskey-drinking German who was a close friend and coworker of my grandfather, Pop Seidel. Both Pop and Charlie Huffman were avid outdoorsmen, spending April through June fishing the trout streams of Pennsylvania and the fall chasing rabbits through the countryside behind Charlie's beagles.

My father loved to tag along with them, eventually maturing enough to participate in their hunting and fishing expeditions. In the spring, they would camp along the trout streams, sleeping on the crushed gravel rock that bordered the railroad tracks, which seemed to hold the warmth of the sun long into the night. Despite this, the night brought freezing temperatures in April and May. Dad and Charlie would sleep on the rocks along the railroad track, while Pop slept more comfortably in the back seat of his 1954 Chevy. My father, mummified in his old wool army-issue sleeping bag, often woke before sunrise. He shivered in the morning frost and looked over at old Charlie sleeping soundly in his sealskin sleeping bag with only his small round face visible, his cheek still packed with tobacco from the night before. Once awake, my father could not fall back to sleep and would lay there, teeth chattering and simply praying for daylight and the morning sun to warm him and thaw out his sore, stiff body.

When Charlie and Pop arose, they kindled the fire and placed a fresh pot of strong black coffee directly on the coals. Charlie fried bacon in a large black cast iron skillet over the open fire, collecting the grease at the bottom of the pan. He cracked a dozen eggs into the bacon grease and fried them sunny side up: two for Dad, two for Pop, and eight for old Charlie Huffman, all five-foot six-inches of him. After the meal, Dad carried the skillet, coffee pot, and utensils to the stream and washed them. Pop packed his pipe with cherry-scented tobacco; Charlie repacked his cheek with a fresh plug of tobacco, fired up a short, fat five-cent cigar, and washed the remnants of his breakfast down with a gulp of cheap whiskey drawn from a stainless steel flask stored in the inner pocket of his sealskin parka. It was barely daylight, breakfast was over, and the group headed down the path through tall, green ferns to the ice-cold water flowing briskly in the clear mountain stream.

"Don't fall in," Charlie yelled as he walked upstream to his favorite pool. "You guys are too much for an old one-armed man to handle!" Charlie Huffman was handicapped, having lost his right arm in a train accident as a teenager. He wore a leather strap across his left shoulder, which draped across his chest. Fastened to the strap was a metal hook in which he would place his rod as he tied fishing knots with his left hand and mouth. The same metal hook also served to stabilize his twenty-gauge shotgun as he aimed at fleeing rabbits running in front of his prized beagles. Charlie was handicapped for lack of a right arm, but was never disadvantaged as a result. He was by far the most successful fisherman my father knew during that era and often made them feel that they were in some strange way handicapped in having two arms interfering with one another. For whatever reason, Charlie was successful at most things he attempted and served as a positive role model and inspiration for those who worked and played with him.

After many hours on the stream, wicker creels full of bright, orange-speckled brook trout lying on a bed of freshly pulled ferns, the fishermen returned to camp and removed their brown rubber hip boots, laying them across the hood of Pop's car, and warmed their cold hands by the smoldering fire. A fresh pot of coffee was brewed, and Charlie began to tell stories, which held my ten-year-old father captive and wide-mouthed as he intently listened.

"Make sure you keep an eye out for the Dungarven Hooper tonight boys, I heard he's patrolling the area. And for God's sake, be sure the water monkeys don't get hold of you!" said Charlie.

It was right at that very moment when my father's heart sank deeper into his chest as his pulse rate climbed precipitously. Not only would he face the cold frost along the railroad tracks after dark, but would also now face the distinct possibility of being captured by water monkeys or kidnapped by the Dungarven Hooper.

"Maybe we oughta go home tonight Charlie," suggested my father. "I think they're callin' for rain in the morning."

"That makes the fishin' all that much better. I'll let you have one of my Muddler Minnow streamer flies, and I'll throw a Black Woolyworm at them," replied Charlie as he choked back another mouthful of whiskey and relit his cigar with a burning stick from the fire. "And besides, I wouldn't think of missin' a chance to rassel with the Dungarven Hooper tonight!"

Chills now reverberated up and down my father's spine as he sank deeper into his sleeping bag and tried not to produce any tears. "Better you than me," replied Dad. "But what if he finds me first?"

"Don't worry about the Dungarven Hooper; he's not after children. I'd be more worried about the water monkeys if I were you. Now get some sleep so you can help with breakfast in the morning."

Charlie suggesting sleep at that moment was like telling my father to go down to the stream, strip down to his skivvies, and go for a midnight swim. It was simply impossible. Images of the Dungarven Hooper filled his thoughts. These images were created over the years by Charlie and Pop Seidel's storytelling along campfires and while traveling throughout the back roads of Pennsylvania. The Dungarven Hooper was a miserable, middle-aged man who wore a black patch over his right eye and a long black trenchcoat. Long brown hair was pulled back from his face and held loosely in a pony-tail falling to mid-back. He drifted the rivers and streams at night on a flat-bottomed, wooden boat relentlessly searching for his lost bride, who was kidnapped shortly after their wedding day, never to be heard from again. Howling out his wife's name in the darkness, he wore a pistol tucked behind his thick, black-leather belt and carried a brass oil lantern in his hand, forever pursuing her captor. Any man who unfortunately approached him would be killed in a most brutal way, his body left to float face down in the river and, like the poor bride of the Dungarven Hooper, never to be heard from again. Children were spared the wrath of the Dungarven Hooper, but were fearful of him nonetheless.

Water monkeys were equally as evil as the Dungarven Hooper, but were less selective as to their victims. They would actually prefer to capture young children because they were lighter and easier to carry as they flew away. Tales of water monkeys began along Pennsylvania trout streams as told to my father by Charlie Huffman, but have evolved and been modified over the years by my father and now by me as I tell the stories to my son James as we sit in a deer stand in South Texas listening for the howl of the water monkeys as they swing through the trees at dusk.

Described by my father as dark-brown furry creatures with long, skinny tails and gray, scaly wings on their backs, water monkeys appear, to me, similar to the flying monkeys enslaved to the Wicked Witch of the West, although were not clothed as they were in the *Wizard of Oz*. Similar in appearance, water monkeys are far meaner than the witch's monkeys and not only were capable of flying, but also lived underwater during the daylight hours. After dark the water monkeys would rise out of the water in search of young children and grab hold of them with their sharp talons and carry them off into the dark night, returning with the victims to their underwater lair. The ultimate fate of the water monkey's victim to this day is unknown, since no one has ever returned after being captured, either alive or dead. My parents would often warn us children to never wander off at the beach after dark, for there was relative safety in numbers, because the water monkeys were sometimes intimidated by large groups, especially when grown-ups were there.

One year when my brother Rob was about nine years old, he questioned everything that came from the mouth of an adult. My father told us the stories of the water monkeys and warned us about their prevalence on Cape Cod beaches. Rob was very skeptical and even mocked our father as he told stories of children, never to be heard from again, after being captured by these creatures.

Later that week, late in the evening on a windy, clear night, my brother Rob realized that he left his puzzle game in the truck. Without asking, he exited the cottage and headed for our truck. Dad warned him about the water monkeys on his way outside, but Rob paid him no mind. Quickly and quietly Dad followed Rob outside and locked the cottage door behind him. Rob, with flashlight in hand, ran to the pick-up, opened the back hatch, and climbed inside to find his puzzle. Dad approached the truck and, with Rob inside, began to rock the truck from side-to-side, knocking my brother off balance and getting his attention. Dad began to howl and shriek in a tone unique to the water monkey and quickly ducked out of sight as Rob's flashlight frantically and erratically scanned the area.

"I know it's you Dad or Ricky, or Mommy, or somebody. You can't fool me." His voice was now less than confident.

Dad retreated to the back side of the cottage and waited for my brother Rob. As Rob scampered up to the door he was surprised to find the door locked. He knocked twice and again began to hear that howling noise that could only be produced by a water monkey. This time the noise was closer and more intense.

"Let me in! Open the door somebody!"

Before the door was opened a hideous howl came closer from behind the cottage, and a large, dark silhouette appeared, hunched over in the shape of a huge monkey. Rob, now hysterical and in tears, was clawing at the door. "Let me in! Let me in! The water monkeys are gonna get me! Let me in!" he screamed as Mom opened the door.

Rob ran into the cottage and right into my mother's arms. He looked as if he had seen a ghost. What he thought he saw was a water monkey coming to take him to the depths of the sea. What he really saw, of course, was Dad trying to teach this little smart-ass a lesson. At the end of the day, Rob was a believer in water monkeys; Dad had finally convinced him of this. In doing so, Dad and Mom now would have an uninvited guest in their bed every night for the next three years on vacation on Cape Cod—like it or not.

lobster

Chapter Eleven

Dad's Titanic

Our week on Cape Cod in the summer of 1993 was spent in early August. Our family rented a friend's old cottage in the national seashore. Although the cottage was small, without a view and in need of repair, it was very isolated and private, completely surrounded by trees, and within walking distance to the ocean beaches. This year would be special in that I would introduce my future wife, Melanie, to the Cape and was excited to show her all the wonderful things this place had to offer. Melanie was raised in a small rice-farming town in south central Texas, the only daughter of a cattle rancher. We met during the second month of my internship at Parkland Hospital in Dallas. She, an Intensive Care Unit nurse, and I, a tired intern, bonded immediately. Before long, she was hearing me tell stories of vacation adventures on the Cape and looked forward to seeing this place for herself. At this time her only points of reference were Mexican and Floridian beaches, as well as the beaches along the Texas Gulf coast.

We spent the first day just driving around making introductions. Melanie was introduced to Ozzie's and Mary Lou's as
we drove along Route 6A heading toward Provincetown. She
was introduced to sweet Wellfleet oysters and a lobster roll at
a bayside restaurant on MacMillan Wharf. We sampled beers
from various local microbreweries at the Chatham Squire as we
awaited our creamy clam chowder and steamer clams. Large
groups of seals lounged on the beach at Monamoy Island as they
waited for the next tide to bring more stripers into the surf for
their consumption. We walked along the beach just above the
water's edge where the sand was still moist but firm, allowing for
easier travel. I pointed out many shells and sea creatures that I had
discovered over the years and hoped Melanie would appreciate.
We sat wrapped in a blanket and watched the orange sun set
over the water and spill its colors all over Race Point beach. That
evening, Melanie experienced two things that I'm sure she'll never
forget. First, she was introduced to the Whitman House restaurant and later introduced to my father's lobster-eating ritual.

The Whitman House is a wonderful eatery and Truro landmark. Located right off Route 6, it was originally established as
an inn in 1894. An Amish carriage sits out front. In the parking
lot, there are often two large center-console fishing boats that
provide much of the fresh seafood on the menu. As you walk
through the front door onto the creaky wooden plank floors,
passing a small pub before entering four large early American

style dining rooms, you are taken back to colonial New England. Above the bar hang mounted striped bass, bluefish, and cod. Nautical artifacts, fishing nets, whaler's harpoons, old sailor's tools, and many old Cape Cod photos cover the walls.

Melanie commented on how cozy this quaint New England restaurant made her feel as we read over the menus. I always enjoy reading through the menus, although I suspect it hasn't changed much over the past twenty years, and I rarely order anything other than boiled lobster, sometimes twins, with a bowl of clam chowder to start. Dad would usually order the King of the Sea—boiled and never cracked three-pound lobster, served with a bowl of clam chowder and a double order of steamers. Dad would repeat this phrase "boiled and never cracked" several times to the waiter before the meal arrived.

"What would you like to drink to start, sir?" asked the waiter to my father.

"I'd like a Beefeater martini on the rocks with a twist of lemon please. And make sure my lobster is not cracked."

"Yes sir, got it," replied the waiter.

As the waiter brought the bread basket to the table and the relish tray was passed, Dad would grab him by the shirt sleeve and quietly ask, "Did you tell the chef to make sure my lobster is not cracked?"

"Yes sir, as you wished," confirmed the waiter, rolling his eyes as he carried bread to the other side of the table.

As we began to pass the salad bowl and waited for our chowder to arrive, Melanie asked what Dad meant by not wanting his lobster cracked.

"You'll see," I said. "Dad loves the juice from inside the lobster's claws and doesn't want the chef to crack open the claws and allow the meat to dry out."

Finally, after bread and relish, creamy cheddar cheese and crackers, clam chowder, two cocktails, a double order of steamer clams, and a salad, the main course arrived. As the waiter tied the plastic lobster bib around Dad's neck, he sat patiently, hungrily staring at the bright red steaming, three-pound carcass lying on the plate in front of him. Ears of corn and a baked potato accompanied the lobster on its plate and were usually eaten first.

As Dad detached the crusher claw at the elbow joint, I gently tapped Melanie's foot to direct her attention to Dad's chair. After the claw was severed, Dad held the large claw up into the air almost as if to worship it and then placed his lips upon the amputation site and slurped the juice from within the claw.

"Mmmmmmmmmmmmmmmmmmm, nectar from the gods!" he exclaimed as he wiped some of the juice from his chin. Embarrassed by Dad's display, we children looked away as if not to encourage him into doing it again, which he did, over and over. The other guests at nearby tables also watched in amazement as Dad guzzled from the lobster claws. Once the large claws were drunk, cracked, and eaten, Dad then focused on the small legs, plucking them individually from the thorax and placing them in between his clenched teeth, stripping them of their meat.

Before long there was nothing left but a disorganized pile of lobster shells, the innards of which were totally extricated and devoured, gills, guts, and all. Antennas and eyeballs were left uneaten. Melanie looked over to me and smiled, now understanding the importance of having an uncracked lobster. To this day, wherever Dad and I order lobster we make sure the waiter understands the importance of not cracking the lobster, and I, too, have acquired the taste for this sweet nectar from the gods.

Dad pushed back and surveyed the rest of the table, knowing he would be responsible for cleaning up any of the other children's uneaten portions. He would soon be eating the remnants of Mom's seafood Newburg, Kristen's filet, and Kim's fish and chips. By default, Dad had eaten the equivalent of two fisherman's platters. At the end of the evening, after coffee and cheesecake, Dad took care of the bill. We thanked our gracious hosts at the door and felt the invigorating snap of cool, crisp night air as we headed back to the cottage for a restful night's sleep.

At the east end of our cottage, there were two bedrooms, side-by-side. Mom and Dad shared the left bedroom, and Melanie would have the right. I would sleep on the couch in the living room and sisters Kristen and Kim would share a pull-out bed in the den. Shortly after falling asleep, I was awakened by Melanie frantically pulling on my arm.

"Rick, wake up, wake up! There's a loud animal outside making a lot of noise! I think it's a bear growling, and it sounds like it might be injured! I can't sleep. I'm scared!"

I sat up and listened to that all-too-familiar growl. It was a sound I've heard many times through the wall that separated my bedroom from my parents at home. It was a sound that I heard as I lay awake next to my father inside our tent in the Adirondack Mountains, or in salmon camp along Canadian rivers. It was the sound of Dad snoring like no one I've ever heard. Dad was without a doubt the grand champion of snoring. He made Curly from the Three Stooges sound like a school girl.

"How could your mom sleep next to that noise for thirty years?" asked Melanie.

"Don't know. She must be desensitized. Maybe she becomes deaf at night."

Melanie sat awake for hours, amazed by the relentless sound that could literally be felt as it could be heard. She finally drifted off to sleep in the den recliner, now buffered by distance from the bedroom. The next morning Dad rose bright and early. He sat at the kitchen table studying the tide chart, sipping his coffee, and finishing a bowl of Raisin Bran. As the rest of the family emerged from their rooms, no one appeared to have had a restful night, especially Mom.

"Richard, you are the loudest snorer I have ever heard," proclaimed Melanie.

"What are you talking about? I never do such a thing. I sleep like a little kitten."

"More like a fierce lion in the process of devouring a wildebeest!"

For the remainder of the trip, Melanie was always prepared for the evening, making a point to get into a deep sleep before my father retired and always wearing earplugs to bed. Back then we referred to this nocturnal noise as "Dad's snoring problem." We now know the medical term to be Obstructive Sleep Apnea, which is not only a nuisance to others, but has serious adverse health implications if not corrected. Happily, Dad faced his accusers and underwent a sleep study, was formally diagnosed, and now wears a night-time breathing apparatus, not only to improve his own health, but to also allow a more restful night to those around him.

After breakfast, on the incoming tide, we trailered our fourteen-foot Glasstron to the Provincetown boat launch. Having received its annual cleaning and a fresh coat of wax prior to vacation, our faded brown fiberglass boat sparkled in the morning sun. All passengers were accounted for: Captain Dad, Mom, Kimberly, Kristen, Melanie, and me. We left a plume of black smoke behind as Dad fired up the motor as we left the harbor and headed out into the bay. Melanie had not experienced anything like this before; in fact, this was her first boat ride in salt water. Emotionally, she was somewhere between apprehensive and terrified, but appeared calm on the outside, other than nearly crushing my hand with her grip. As she looked back toward the green and beige landscape sandwiched between dark-blue water and ice-blue sky, her apprehensions eased. She was now experiencing what I described to her back in Texas. There is nothing more pacifying than a calm, sunny day on the water in Cape Cod Bay.

As Dad positioned our boat in about twenty feet of water, with wind direction to move us toward the mainland into shallow water, I baited our rods with sand eels and placed squid strips on fluke rigs—shiny silver spinners with intervening red and green beads. Before long we were catching fluke, one after another. Melanie, never before a fisherman, began to enjoy battling the fish. She even learned to properly bait her own hook. As she looked over the side of the boat, Melanie commented on how clear the water was, as she could easily see white clam shells lying on the bottom in twenty feet of water. That view was occasionally interrupted by schools of sand eels as they passed under our boat. Fleeing from their pursuers below, the sand eels create clouds of shimmering silver flashes in the water as the sun reflects off their sides. As they are pushed closer to the surface, they are spotted by terns, and the dive bombing attack begins. With the terns diving close to our boat, we knew we were into fish.

Mom sat in the back of the boat, Diet Coke in hand, simply enjoying the day. Nothing gives her more pleasure than being around her children.

"Make sure you don't hurt those fish when you release them, Ricky," Mom would always say. She is an animal lover at heart and hates to see any creature suffer, even feeling sorry for the dead sand eels that baited our hooks.

"Don't worry Mom, he's much happier now that the hook is *out* of his mouth. He'll be fine."

Needless to say, it was always difficult keeping a few fish for dinner when Mom was on board. The image of a fish slowly dying in our live well broke her heart.

After catching and releasing nearly thirty fluke, the wind direction changed and we began to drift out into deeper water. In sixty feet, Dad's fish finder lit up like a Christmas tree and began to chirp nonstop. We knew a large school of fish swam under our boat, but did not know the species.

"Get ready boys and girls, they're in here thick. I can smell 'em! Work those jigs!" Dad proclaimed.

Within three minutes, we hooked three fish. The fish did not fight like bluefish and never came to the surface behind the boat. Instead, they stayed deep under the boat with a steady pull on the line and occasional head shake. As one of the fish neared the boat, its gray and white body and unmistakable silhouette revealed the species identity—sandshark. As I boated the first one, removing the hook from its jaw with pliers and held it toward Melanie, she commented on how cute the little toothy critter was. I knew different. Although these shark species are only thirty to forty inches in length on average, they are well-designed, armored beasts. Having a skeleton constructed exclusively of cartilage, they are contortionists, able to flex their spine 360 degrees. With this ability to touch nose to tail, the unfortunate soul holding one by the tail alone will quickly experience sharp cutting teeth tearing at his hand. Additionally, sharp spikes on the front side of the dorsal fin and tail serve to pierce and tear the flesh. With mere slits for pupils in a yellow iris, they even look evil as they stare back at you defiantly with their cat eyes. Before long, Melanie was convinced that theses creatures were no longer *cute*.

That same afternoon, Melanie would be introduced to two other evil creatures, much smaller than the sandsharks, but equally as capable of inflicting pain. As we drifted in the bay later that afternoon, the bright orange sun dropped toward the horizon and the gentle breeze that moved our boat over the schools of fish subsided.

"Ouch, something bit me!" yelled Melanie. "It got me again, I'm bleeding! What is it?"

I quickly swatted the beast as it landed a third time on her shoulder. It fell to the floor of the boat, lying on its back, stunned but not dead. Before the beast could right itself, I crushed it with the sole of my flip-flop.

"Green-headed deer fly," I replied. "We better head in to shore. Where there's one, they'll be many and we have no wind to keep them away. Let's head in Dad."

Before we were underway, more attacks ensued. The female green-headed deer fly (*Tabanus americanus Forester*) is a vicious, painful biter with knife-like mouth parts. They are light brown in color with large bright green eyes and reddish-brown thorax and abdomen. They live around salt marshes and, after laying their first set of eggs, search for warm-blooded animals. Blood provides them with protein used to develop their eggs. They are attracted to dark objects, particularly the color blue. They are fairly resistant to pesticides and the only good defense is a swift swat of the hand or simple avoidance. Melanie quickly learned that she was no match for these demons.

The second evil creature lay waiting for us back at the water's edge. As we pulled into the harbor, Dad approached a mooring just beyond the boat ramp. We were fortunate this year to have a mooring available. Dad had befriended a Provincetown policeman who offered his mooring for the week. This was extremely convenient in that we would not have to trailer our boat to and from the launch every day, avoiding the narrow, crowded streets of Provincetown. Always a gentleman, Dad pulled into shallow water near shore to allow the women to depart from the boat. We then drove out about 100 yards and secured our boat to the mooring, now in about four feet of water. In order not to disturb Mom, we quickly filleted our catch, jumped over the side carrying our fish, and walked in to shore. I looked back to see gulls splashing down onto the water, devouring the remnants of the fluke carcasses that we left floating there for them. As we neared the shore, sun now sitting on top of the water, we saw the girls jumping up and down on shore, swatting their hands in the air.

"Hurry up, something is attacking us!" yelled Kim.

We soon walked into an invisible cloud of vicious microscopic flies called no-see-ems. These are biting gnats that can barely be seen and come out near the water's edge toward dusk. They are relentless flies that hurt worse than mosquitoes and attack in swarms, making you feel as though a thousand invisible darts are being launched into your skin. The only method of escape is to get away from the water and into the safety of a vehicle, which is what we did, as we scratched at our wounds.

"Sharks have nothing on these bugs," said Melanie. "I thought Texas mosquitoes were bad. These bugs make mosquitoes look like chickadees."

As we drove back to the cottage, the weather turned sour, and a steady rain began to fall. The forecasters predicted a cold front and rain for the next three days. Unfortunately, they were correct. Our boat, although conveniently tied to a mooring in the Provincetown Harbor, was left open without a cover. It sat there helpless, welcoming the rain, but without a bilge pump or any other means to bail itself. For the next three days, we partook in indoor activities in order to keep Melanie interested and to prevent her and Mom from sinking into a "slough of despond." We visited the sights, Mom took us to visit her friends at the fudge shop, and we heard many of Dad's Cape Cod stories.

By the afternoon of the third day, weather still gray and rainy, Dad and I decided to check on the boat. Mom and Melanie accompanied us to the boat launch parking lot. What we found there was startling, but in retrospect, should not have been unexpected. Now, at high tide, we found our boat nearly sunk. From steering wheel to stern, our beloved 14-foot Glasstron was under water, motor completely submerged and not visible. The bow line remained tied to the mooring and only about three feet of our boat remained dry and afloat. Still raining, with thunder and lightening in the distance, on an incoming tide, we had to act quickly. With some of our coolers now floating away from the boat, Dad and I decided to swim out to the boat in order to salvage some of our equipment. We knew that the heavy tackle boxes were still likely anchored to the floor of the boat and the rods were safely stored in the side wells, while the boat cushions and lighter items had likely already floated off.

Dad, wearing khaki long pants and a white tee shirt, removed his shoes and socks, handed his watch, wallet, and keys to my tearful mother and headed out to sea. I, now realizing the danger and urgency of the situation, followed. Melanie tried to grab my arm and make me come to my senses, but my adrenaline levels were too high. I was covered in goose bumps, shaking as I entered the cold water, already soaking wet from the rain. However, I was too numb to feel pain as I focused on saving our vessel.

The water quickly deepened in the high tide and two-foot waves rhythmically crashed against us as our journey to the boat transitioned from a walk to a swim. The water temperature was clearly warmer than the air, so the deeper it became, the less I trembled. Melanie and Mom stood on the boat ramp arm-in-arm worried sick about our fate. I'm sure Melanie was recalling our fishing trip three days before, where we were catching unlimited quantities of evil sharks from these same waters. Was it now time for them to seek revenge on her future husband and father-in-law?

Dad and I are both good swimmers and quickly arrived at the boat. Dad instinctively, but mistakenly, tried to climb into the boat for reasons I still do not understand. Forgetting all laws of physics that would warn against adding more weight to a partially submerged vessel, Dad grabbed hold of the mooring line and threw his leg over the side of the boat. Now attempting to transfer his weight, the boat took on many more gallons of water and turned on its side, and Dad plunged back into the bay.

"Aaaaaaahhhhhhhhhhhhrrrrrrrrrrrrrrrrrr!" he yelled in frustration. "I'm going to swim to the marina for help. You stay here with the boat."

Having just violated a major law of physics, Dad now violated one of the most time-honored laws of mariner ethics. In all cases of sinking marine vessels, the captain is to go down with the ship. I, as first mate, should have been elected to swim off for help. Instead I was left treading shark-infested water, fighting hypothermia in a torrential downpour alongside my beloved sinking boat, and watching cushions and coolers float away. With thunder rumbling in the distance, I looked back at the boat ramp to see Mom and Melanie still huddled together under an umbrella staring back at me. I began to realize that I was probably now safer out here in the water, for there would be serious ramifications with them over the emotional stress Dad and I were inducing.

With all the fury of Marc Spitz butterflying his way to the finish line, Dad was now swimming full bore toward Flyers Marina, about a half mile to the west.

"Try to save the coolers!" he yelled back to me as he stopped to catch his breath.

"Save your own damn coolers," I mumbled under my breath as thoughts of mutiny now filled my head. With teeth chattering and fingertips now shriveled like dried prunes, I contemplated abandoning ship and swimming back to shore to the comfort of a nice warm blanket and heated car. I was only 100 yards from shore and in no more than twelve feet of water, but with rain pouring down, I felt as though I was lost at sea. Treading water, then grabbing hold of the mooring to rest intermittently, I knew I needed to stay with the boat, despite Melanie's encouragement to swim to shore. As I stayed out there, scenes from Peter Benchley's

Jaws began to fill my mind, a film made not far away in the Nantucket Sound. Despite Melanie's fears, I knew sandsharks were no threat, but knowing that there were other more dangerous species inhabiting these cold waters made my heart race. Blue sharks, Great Whites, and Makos were common to these waters, and I began to see images of me being abruptly pulled underwater only to surface in a pool of red.

As Dad's splashing silhouette became smaller in the distance, just when all hope was nearly lost, our salvation arrived. Not in the form of divine intervention, a returning lobsterman, or even a Coast Guard rescue unit, our salvation was in the form of three gay scuba divers.

Suddenly, from nowhere, a gray rubber raft came upon me containing three muscular, dark mustached men resembling Freddie Mercury. Instead of leather pants and black leather vest, they were wearing wet suits, scuba masks, and tanks and offered me a tow. Realizing that my captain was out of pocket, I made the executive decision to accept their offer and climbed into their raft. Shaking violently in the cold wet air, I wrapped myself in a towel as they released our boat from the mooring and tied it to the back ring on their raft. Heavy with water, our old brown boat was slowly towed to the beach alongside the boat ramp.

Uncle Carl, called earlier by Mom, now arrived and was briefed on the situation. He thanked the scuba divers for their heroism and handed them a twenty dollar bill for their trouble.

Melanie called Flyers Marina, instructing them to call off the rescue and send my father back to his salvaged vessel. As the tide began to recede, we stood alongside our boat, filled with sand and seaweed. Gallons of oil and gasoline-stained water sat stagnant in the bottom of the boat, about twelve inches deep. Although most of the boat was on dry land, the stern was still submerged, not allowing us to simply pull the plug and allow the water to drain from the hull. We would have to hand bail the water from the boat. We took all rods, tackle boxes, fish finder, and other equipment from the boat, loaded it into the back of the pick-up truck, and washed and flushed everything with clean fresh water. My father, wrapped in his own beach towel, had now arrived back at the boat launch. Now wearing his long-beaked fishing cap and dark brown sunglasses, he assumed his role as captain, thanking me for my efforts to save our boat. He offered me a promotion, but I could move no higher as I was already first mate.

"I'll move you to Assistant-to-the-Captain, which is one notch above first mate. I'm afraid your mother and Melanie may be facing demotions, perhaps even down to lowly deck-scrubbers, for not helping with the rescue. Now Carl, help us get this boat bailed out."

"You're lucky I don't get on the next plane back to Texas and leave you and your son here for the sharks, Richard!" barked Melanie. "You are *risk-takers*, and you've just taken about ten years off my life!"

I tried to reassure my future wife that things were fine, we were all safe, and this was not an uncommon occurrence here on the Cape. That only made things worse, and Melanie and Mom decided to get out of the rain and go back to the cottage. We assured them that we would bail out the boat, call Flyers Marina to come and get our boat, dry out the motor and get it running again, and then be home for dinner.

Uncle Carl volunteered to begin bailing and was handed our portapotty—a one gallon plastic milk jug with a hole cut in the side. This very same vessel had provided relief to many a diuresing male fisherman over the years. Standing knee deep in the harbor alongside the boat, Uncle Carl dipped his hand into the boat to scoop out his first jug of water. Long, thin, blue lightning bolts emerged from the water, striking Carl in the hand. He rapidly withdrew his hand, dropping the jug on the way out.

"Ouch!"

"What's wrong Carl?" asked Dad. "Crab got hold of your toe?"

"Rich, the battery is still connected and I got shocked when I put my hand in the water."

"C'mon Carl, no excuses. Don't make me have to demote you, too. Take the pain! Take the pain! We have to get this boat bailed out before dark."

Carl reluctantly tried again and again, each time yelling out as his hand was shocked as it entered the water. Before long, his hair nearly standing on end, Uncle Carl gave up and offered my father the jug.

"Here, Rich. Demotion or no demotion, I can't take it any-more. It's your turn."

"Are you crazy, man? After seeing what has happened to you? I'm not that foolish. I don't want to become a fatality! We'll come back in low tide, release the plug and let the water drain out."

"Aye-aye captain."

Late afternoon was now upon us, and the weather was starting to clear. We decided to leave our boat at rest here on the beach and return tomorrow during low tide to drain the remainder of the water. Looking out over the bay, we could see clouds clearing, allowing columns of sunlight to break through and brighten the dark gray water. The rain slowed to a mist. Instead of going right back to the cottage as we promised, the brighter weather infused our minds with thoughts of outdoor activities, as we had been confined for the past three days.

With low tide approaching, I asked, "How 'bout we go and dig up some steamers for dinner?"

"Sure. Nothing like a fresh pot of steamers on a cold, rainy day," replied Dad. "Let's go."

We left our boat and climbed into Dad's pick-up. Arriving at Pamet Harbor we found very few vehicles in the lot. Puddles remained in the parking lot, but the black asphalt began to dry. Swishy greeted us in the lot, and we sat on the tailgait and shared a cold beer.

"What are you guys doin' out here on such a miserable day?" he asked.

"Hoping for the weather to change."

"I know what you mean. Nobody's been out here last three days. Even the commercial guys stayed home."

For the commercial fishermen to stay home, meant that the weather must have really been dangerous. Dad went on to tell of our boat sinking, which evoked a sarcastic laugh from old Swishy.

"Dammit man! You guys been comin' up here for how long and you sink your boat when it's tied to a mooring in the harbor?! You need to put an automatic bailer into that boat of yours. That is if you want to keep it. Ha!"

Swishy walked away as Dad just shook his head, looking as though he felt defeated. I'm sure he regretted telling Swishy that story, seeing himself demoted in Swishy's mind. We grabbed our gloves, bucket, and clam rakes and headed to the clam beds. The Pamet is a river that rises and falls with the tides. Now only shin deep in dead low tide, we crossed over to the marshy creek channels on the flats. With each step in the river many sand eels would emerge and quickly disappear under the sand, fleeing our footsteps. On the other side of the river we walked across thousands of opened shells—clam, mussels, and oysters— all having previously been devoured by sea birds, and then we disappeared into the tall green marsh grass. We soon came upon narrow creek channels, most now dry with some pooled water in the deeper spots.

"Look for the holes and then start diggin' boys."

Dad instructed us on how to locate steamer beds. Small holes in the wet sand served to mark the clam beds below, some up to a foot deep. We gently started to dig with our hands or rake until the shiny white, oval-shaped clams were unearthed. They are also called soft shell clams and, as their name implies, need to be carefully handled so that their shells are not cracked. Within an hour we collected a bucketful and headed back to the truck.

"We'll soak them in a little corn meal overnight to release the sand from inside and then cook them up for lunch tomorrow," said Dad. "Let's pickup some mussels in the river on the way back."

As we crossed the river we collected a few clumps of dark-blue mussels to steam along with the clams. The truck was loaded, and we headed out of the parking lot onto Depot Road.

It was nearly 7:00 P.M. when we pulled alongside the cottage. We opened the door to find Mom and Melanie sitting at the kitchen table, phonebook open, calling every hospital and medical clinic from Provincetown to Boston. They were convinced that we were injured or worse, perhaps drowned in the harbor, struck by lightening or involved in a traffic accident on our way back from the boat launch.

"Where have you been, we were worried sick," asked Melanie.

"Digging clams. We got some really nice steamers and mussels for lunch tomorrow. Is there any corn meal in the cabinet?" I responded, now becoming aware of their anger.

For the next thirty minutes Dad and I listened to lectures from both Melanie and Mom about responsibility, concern for others, the dangers of swimming in rough water during a thunderstorm, risk-taking, etc. To this day, now fifteen years later, I am reminded about this incident by Melanie whenever I am about to take the kids out into the ocean in our boat, or any other place without her being there to supervise. I always acknowledge my errors in judgment and respond with a "Yes, dear." But under my breath as I look back on these times with fond memories, laughter, and valuable lessons learned, I whisper "No risk, no reward."

tuna

Chapter Twelve

MacMillan Wharf

There are few places I enjoy visiting more on Cape Cod than MacMillan Wharf. It's been a regular destination year after year, not only as a place to park our vehicle for easy access into Provincetown, but also simply a place to stroll around and enjoy the sights on the pier. The wharf, now refurbished and converted from an old wooden frame to its current concrete and metal structure, provides the framework for a carnival of sailing vessels and activities. It serves as home to the more than century-old Provincetown fishing fleet and not only connects land to sea, but also connects Provincetown to its past.

Provincetown, established as a town in 1727, was first visited by European explorers in 1602, although likely sheltered Viking explorers years earlier. The *Mayflower Compact* was signed by the Pilgrims in its harbor in 1620, before they traveled across the bay to establish their settlement in Plymouth. In 1700 the first permanent settlement was established, but it wasn't until after the Revolutionary War when the population began to grow significantly and Provincetown flourished into the main maritime and fishing center on Cape Cod.

During the Civil War, Portuguese sailors were recruited by American ships in the Azores and Cape Verde Islands for their crews, later to establish homes in Provincetown. The Portuguese community remains strong to this day because of immigrants to this area during the nineteenth century, coming to work on whaling vessels and fishing boats. By the mid to late 1800s Provincetown became one of the greatest and busiest seaports in the country, and the Provincetown fishing fleet grew to over 700 vessels.

By the early twentieth century, after the Portland Gale of 1898 decimated the fishing industry as it destroyed many of the town's wharves, Provincetown became more of an artistic community, much as it is today. In my eyes, there is a wonderful balance between past and present, land and sea, art and the harsh reality of nature's forces.

Today, MacMillan Wharf is one of only a few surviving wharves, where there once was fifty-six. Train tracks once ran from the center of town out onto the wharf where whale oil, baleen, and whalebone was loaded and shipped to the mainland.

Its namesake is Admiral Donald B. "Dan, Cap'n Mac" MacMillan (1874-1970), one of America's greatest Arctic explorers. Born in Provincetown, son of a sea captain and shipbuilder's daughter, he was destined to live on the sea, despite early child-hood tragedy. His father, Captain Neil MacMillan, was lost at sea during a gale off the coast of Newfoundland in 1883, and his mother Sarah Gardner MacMillan, soon followed her husband in death in 1886. After adoption by another sea captain, he helped support the family by selling cranberries and skinning dogfish and later moved to Freeport, Maine where he completed high school. With a strong work ethic, Dan MacMillan paid his way through college, graduating from Bowdoin in 1898. It was here that he met Admiral Robert E. Peary and was invited to serve on his expedition to discover the North Pole in 1909. This became Cap'n Mac's calling. On his eighty-eight-foot wooden schooner, *Bowdoin,* he would lead 26 voyages into the Arctic between 1921 and 1954, his last at age eighty. He has made significant con-tributions to the advancement of knowledge in many different areas of Arctic exploration including oceanography, archaeology, botany, meteorology, glaciology, and anthropology. He was made commander of arctic expeditions during World War II and re-ceived the Congressional Medal of Honor in 1944. Despite all of his accomplishments and accolades, he remained a humble man, befitting the old, strong, historic wharf that to this day survives and bears his name.

As you walk out over the water on MacMillan Wharf, long, narrow catwalks descend from the sides of the pier down to float-ing docks, which serve as berths for a variety of sailing vessels.

The docks are secured to large concrete blocks on the harbor's bottom by heavy rusted chains and thick rope, becoming draped with seaweed as they penetrate the clear water. The dark-brown wooden pilings that support the wharf are covered with mussels, barnacles, and seaweed just below the waterline. Depending on which catwalk you descend, you can be taken for various maritime adventures. Tall wooden sailing schooners such as the *Hindu* or the *Bay Lady II* take you across the bay for a relaxing cruise with bright masts full of the wind, as was done by similar ships two hundred years ago.

Tourists gather daily, standing in line to board the *Dolphin*, *Portuguese Princess*, or *Captain Red*, large whale-watching ships, to be carried offshore to Stellwagen Bank in hopes of seeing whales dance on the ocean's surface. Humpback, Finback, and Minke whales are common to this area, which serves as their summer feeding ground. I have many fond memories standing at the rail in awe of these huge mammals, amazed by their size and grace. Identified by specific markings and scars, the whales are known by the crew individually and given names, returning from the Caribbean to these waters every summer, year after year. The Humpback's feeding ritual is a sight to behold. Diving deep below the surface, the whale positions itself below a school of sand eels. As it ascends, it releases a spiral column of air bubbles through its blowhole, which serves to concentrate and confuse the baitfish. The water below them now changes from deep blue to pale jade in color as the whale approaches from below. A large baitball is formed as the eels congregate at the surface, and the whale emerges with jaws wide open, capturing thousands in a single pass. Two more passes are made, every time, one right after the other, until the whale gracefully descends into the depths, its huge tail arching up and then down as if to say good-bye for now. Its only footprint left is that of an oval oil slick on the surface and bits of baitfish, now being scavenged by sea birds.

Farther down the wharf, charter captains stand on their decks retying lines after a long day's fishing for stripers and blues, sometimes offshore for tuna. Outriggers now secured alongside the tower, the boats are tied by thick ropes attached to the cleats on the dock. Large orange and pink balls hang over the gunwale to cushion the fiberglass boat hulls from the wooden dock. Successful fisherman pose for photos with their trophy fish as deckhands filet the rest of their catch and hose down the bloody entrails from the dock. In late August and September, it's not uncommon to see a giant bluefin tuna hanging from a wench by its tail over the back of one of these charter boats, with proud captain standing next to a catch that miniaturizes him. Next to his charter boat, submerged just under the surface, hangs his large, circular metal fish trap containing nervous bluefish (future tuna bait) continually swimming the perimeter of the trap, anxiously awaiting their next trip. Nailed to the wooden piling next to his boat are several old tuna tails displayed as trophies, evidence of prior successful trips. With rod and reel or harpoon, the successful tuna captain will fetch nearly a year's earnings from the carcass of a "Giant," an almost thousand-pound fish. This is thanks to the rising demand of the Japanese for sushi and dramatically falling international stocks of tuna. Unfortunately, "Giants" have become rare, and much smaller because of worldwide overfishing.

Captain Bill and the *Cee Jay*, large party boats, sit on their berths after returning from fluke fishing in the bay. These boats are often full of inexperienced tourists, many of whom have not fished previously. With anglers dropping baited hooks over the side into the current, standing elbow-to elbow at the rail, much of the mates' time is spent untangling knotted lines, or cleaning vomit from queasy landlubbers. I am not too embarrassed to confess that my father, uncles, and I have spent several afternoon trips with Captain Bill, usually when our boat was under repair in the boatyard or out of commission from a mishap. Desperate times called for desperate measures, but the Captain Bill and Cee Jay are fixtures on the wharf, providing many tourists with wonderful fishing memories.

Many smaller private boats, yachts, and sailboats sit tied to the docks along MacMillan Wharf and its parallel pier to the north. Their owners enjoy a cocktail on the deck before heading into P-town for dinner. Electrical cords recharge their ship's batteries before heading off to the next port. Some fathers teach their children how to jig for mackerel and small harbor bass in the shade under the pier. Next to this pier, adjacent to a large mooring field, sits a small wooden dock, rubber tires nailed to its sides to protect boat hulls from its sharp corners. Often a challenge to gently approach in high wind, this is where refueling takes place. Long gas lines repel from the pumps on the pier, thirty feet above. An elderly Portuguese man stands there, looking down upon you, waiting for the order.

"How much gas you want? Make sure you use the blue-handled pump, red is diesel."

After the tanks are full, a small blue plastic bucket is lowered by rope and the cash is laid down, covered by a flat lead weight.

"Have a good day, fellas."

Three hundred yards from the end of MacMillan Wharf lies a breakwater, which serves to protect this placid water from high seas blown in off the ocean. Constructed in 1972 of huge granite boulders, it measures 2500 feet long, by sixteen feet tall, by ten feet wide. Its top is covered with the black and white excrement from resting seagulls, appearing as though a neauveaux artist had splattered it with paint. A foghorn perched on the wall warns nighttime travels of its presence. Its deep baritone bellow sounds like a bass viol as a bow is slowly drawn across its thickest string. As night draws near, black sea ducks float on the calm water, periodically disappearing under the surface to return with a fish in their bill.

Near the end of the wharf at the Whydah Pirate Museum, large ferry boats collect passengers traveling to and from Boston.

Inside the museum, there are all sorts of trinkets and treasures for the kids, and many books about old pirate ships and shipwrecks. The Whydah was the first pirate ship ever discovered in North America, found in 1983 off the coast of Wellfleet, a town about ten miles west of Provincetown. Heavy with treasure stolen from at least fifty-three other ships, it ran aground off Cahoon Hollow in a storm in April 1717. There were only two survivors out of a crew of 148.

On the west end of the wharf the remnants of the once 700-vessel Provincetown fishing fleet sit at rest, now numbering less than twenty. Large iron and wooden trawlers, also known as draggers, battered and rusted, await their next voyage to sea. A green net wrapped around a large spool perched at the stern still holds shells and starfish from prior trips. The pilothouse toward the bow is dark and cluttered. Even the more recently painted trawlers show their age with rust stains and black diesel soot bleeding over their brighter colored sides. Some trawlers will be off-loading their catch, as tired, unshaved mates fill plastic carts with fish from down in their hulls, to be hoisted by crane into refrigerated tractor trailers for processing. Other mates will be welding or darning the dragger's nets in preparation for the next trip. The fishermen here are quiet, talking with each other, not mingling much with the tourists, for theirs is one of the most dangerous professions and must be taken seriously. I am always respectful of the Provincetown fishing fleet. All of them have lost friends and family members, generations past, to the harsh realities of the sea. As I walk in between these ships along the docks that separate them, there is the familiar smell of dead fish, oil, and diesel fumes. Gulls and pigeons walk the decks and roost on the masts, looking for scraps.

Looking up toward the sky, I'm struck by the number of flags, all colors and shapes of triangles and rectangles, flying from flagpoles on the wharf as well as ships' masts. Made of nylon and plastic, they crack and ripple in the stiff wind. Overhead, gulls hover, wings spread, effortlessly drifting on the wind current like kites.

As I walk back to the mainland, I look over the side into the clear water to see minnows swimming over a sandy bottom laden with shells and starfish. Even tiny hermit crabs can be seen dancing across the bottom. Ambitious adolescents dive for quarters thrown from the pier by curious tourists. I look back toward town to see small boats anchored in the shallows and wooden skeletons of old piers from days past sporadically breaking up the coastline. In the background, the Pilgrim Monument stands 350 feet above the town, its four gargoyles looking down onto the Outer Cape in all directions. The green landscape provided by shade trees over narrow streets is broken up by white church steeples, welcoming us home from the sea.

tern

Chapter Thirteen

Close Quarters

From 1994 our family has grown because of marriages and grandchildren, requiring larger rental properties to house us. We've always planned our vacations together so aunts, uncles, and cousins could reunite here once a year. While our extended family, in the 1970s and 1980s, could fill a few bayside cottages, it now requires at least three or four homes. This is often more challenging to arrange and places us in more varied locations throughout the town. Despite larger homes, we stay in close quarters.

Building covenants restrict the size of most Truro homes to three or four small bedrooms. Therefore, other areas of the house such as dens, living rooms, and bonus rooms are converted into makeshift bedrooms. Furniture is rearranged, air mattresses inflated, and sleeping bags unrolled. There is a hierarchy in the house just as on the boat and with age comes seniority. Mom and Dad always have their own bedrooms; what is left is delegated based on the size of our individual clans. Kristen, Kim, and their husbands, the youngest with fewest children, usually sleep on the floor in the den and living room. Uncle Bob, wrapped in his World War II wool army sleeping bag, slumbers on the couch. Dad often sits alone on the back patio or deck, enjoying water views and birdlife, trying to escape the mayhem raised by young children in the house. He often appears deep in thought, reflecting on past times and probably wondering how many more summers he has left to enjoy this place.

At home, we all have a lot of personal space that, on vacation, is sacrificed and often invaded. Close quarters sometimes become crammed quarters, and patience and compromise become mandatory. Conflicts arise, debate ensues, sometimes leading to argument, often over small, seemingly insignificant things. One such incident occurred over a simple hall light. Uncle Bob and Dad were dorming in adjacent rooms separated by a narrow hallway. After Dad had fallen asleep, Uncle Bob got up and turned the hall light on, illuminating Dad's room and startling him. Dad sternly lashed out, using some four-letter explicatives, and demanded that the light be turned off. The next morning there was some obvious tension at the breakfast table. Both arguments were heard. Uncle Bob defended himself by stating that light was necessary in the event that someone got up to use the bathroom in the middle of the night. With stairs close by, surely someone would have an accident in the dark. Dad then responded in a "Johnny Cochran-esque" style, stating that the light was unnecessary and, in fact, was only serving to attract dangerous insects such as mosquitoes and pinching bugs into the area, which would prey on sleeping victims. Furthermore, Dad argued that Uncle Bob's motives were ingenuine and motivated by his own secondary intentions. Dad revealed that Uncle Bob suffered from arachnophobia and was using the light to ward off nocturnal spiders in pursuit of his own blood. We were reminded of a traumatic incident that occurred in Uncle Bob's life several years previously. While working for General Motors and living in Allentown, Uncle Bob discovered a large spider crawling toward him on the arm of his recliner. Using a rolled-up newspaper as a club he squashed the spider with one swift strike. Thinking nothing of his action, he crumpled the smeared carcass into a tissue and flushed it down the commode. Before retiring later that evening, he noticed a large spider similar in appearance to the one he killed earlier. It appeared to be staring at him defiantly, motionless on the wall. The next morning, Uncle Bob noticed a burning discomfort along the right side of his neck. While shaving he spotted a red, raised area with two small puncture marks on his right neck, just overlying the jugular vein. Convinced he was attacked in the middle of the night by the dead spider's vengeful mate, he had the apartment fumigated that day. Forevermore, Uncle Bob has a strong dislike and fear of spiders, sleeping with the light on in unfamiliar environments.

At the end of the day, a deal was struck that accommodated both Dad and Uncle Bob. This one simple debate and revelation of Uncle Bob's arachnophobia, and Dad's fear of pinching bugs, has served as fodder for many subsequent practical jokes involving rubber insects placed in strategic locations.

Over the years, many of us have been victims of practical jokes as well as overt harassment during these weeks in close quarters. I, being a gastroenterologist, am often the "butt" of many jokes launched at me by my siblings. Most of my family—outside of medicine—have no clue what my job entails, having images of me as Ed Norton from the *Honeymooners* climbing down into the bowels of humanity and shoveling shit all day. I try to defend myself by enlightening them with stories of heroic life-saving procedures using the most advanced technology, often saving patients from much more invasive and morbid surgeries, controlling severe hemorrhaging, and curing or preventing cancers. To no avail, my family, especially younger siblings, are much more interested to hear what sort of foreign bodies I've extracted from a schizophrenic's stomach or rectum lately, or how many times I've been vomited upon in the last month. I've learned by now that efforts to defend my chosen profession are futile and I laugh out loud along with them.

Many of us have also been subject to victimization by practical jokesters. The video camera has further enabled long-lasting images of embarrassing moments to be replayed over and over again. One night my mother fell into a deep sleep on the couch. While most of us were in bed asleep, brother Rob, always an opportunist when it comes to mischief, and preying on Mom's reputation as a "junk-food addict," scattered all sorts of goodies around my mother's makeshift bed. Cup cakes, candy wrappers, potato chip bags, soft drink cans, half-eaten donuts were cluttered all around her. With video camera in hand, Rob documented the scene. The next morning, Mom awoke to the mess, unaware of what had happened. At breakfast the video was played for all to see. Mom was accused of sleep-walking in the middle of the night and going on an eating binge. Demanding further video evidence of the actual act, not just the post-production video, she suspected foul play, but made Rob promise never to show the video to any of her friends or coworkers. Dad's snoring has been well-documented in a similar fashion.

Most nights we gather together at the largest house for dinner, or after eating out, to share stories and laughs over cocktails. Our children get to reintroduce themselves to their cousins, who they only see a few times a year. The house is packed; chairs from other parts of the house are brought into the great room. We men share the same fishing stories told year after year, sometimes adding new ones to the list. Often politics are discussed, usually leading to heated arguments. The younger generation sits at the table playing cards and board games, while the women supervise the children, laughing at their funny antics. As the hands on the clock pass midnight, the party starts to break up and plans are made for the next day.

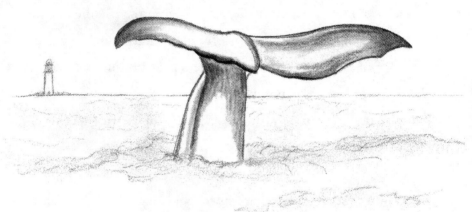

Humpback whale off Race Point

Chapter Fourteen

Camping

In the summer of 1980, as Ronald Reagan challenged President Jimmy Carter for the White House, soon to achieve a landslide victory in November, our family was about to experience one of the most unique and memorable vacations of all time. As the decade of the 1970s ended, it left us with a poor economy, high interest rates, inflation, high taxes, and the highest gasoline prices in history. It was also a time when my parents saw their older children attending college in the not-too-distant future. Financial preparations for the future were necessary, leading my mother back into the work force, gaining employment as a night-time admissions clerk at the local hospital, from 3:00 P.M. until 11:00 P.M. This required sacrifice from the entire family. I would serve as babysitter after school until my father returned from work around 5:30 P.M. I would also be responsible for reheating dinner previously prepared by Mom before she left for work. Dad would often work a second job at night, although side-jobs were not as available during these years. Most people would not spend money to improve their house, when they had to spend so much on oil to heat it. Despite all the hardship, my parents still found a way to get us to the Cape that summer. However, our lodging was much different. Instead of a warm, dry, cozy cottage on the beach, we would spend our week in a six-man, blue canvas tent.

The Coastal Acres Campground is located in a wooded section of Provincetown, conveniently within walking distance of downtown, adjacent to the Cape Cod National Seashore with its majestic dunes, quiet bike trails, and horseback riding stables nearby. At twelve dollars a night per campsite, it was a bargain. I'm sure that was the main factor behind my parents' decision to camp.

We arrived that year, again in Dad's GMC farm truck with boat in tow, packed to the gills with children, luggage, fishing gear, food, and plenty of bug spray. This year, additional camping equipment was included: a blue canvas tent rolled-up with aluminum support poles and ground spikes stuffed inside. An old, green Coleman propane stove, rusted and scarred from prior camping adventures, served to cook our meals and warm our hands in the cool, damp mornings in camp. Dad's college friends, Phyllis and Emil, along with their four children, joined us this year at the campground, as they had done on many previous summers at the Cape. Instead of a tent, Emil arrived with a hard-top camper trailored to his wood-paneled station wagon. My father and Emil have been close friends since business school at Wilkes College. They share many common interests, but are quite different in many ways. The analogy that comes to mind is that of Homer Simpson and his next-door neighbor, Ned Flanders. I mean no disrespect to either party with this comparison. Like Homer, my father was overweight, strongly opinionated, sometimes loud and argumentative, enjoyed donuts and an occasional beer (Old Milwaukee instead of Duff) and faced adversity head-on, many times getting knocked on his ass but always getting right back on his feet, dusting off, and moving forward. Unlike Homer, my father was highly intelligent with a better vocabulary (although sometimes using four-letter expletives instead of "doh!"), never choked his children, did not have alopecia, and did not marry a skinny woman with tall blue hair. Emil, like Ned, was extremely well organized and neat. His camper and station wagon, although also packed to the gills like our truck, was loaded in such a manner that everything was in its proper place and could be found easily. Emil was always prepared for emergencies with tool boxes, flashlights, and medical supplies packed into a black "fanny-pack" strapped to his belt alongside his camera case and leatherman's tool. Like Ned, he was well-spoken, calm, never raised his voice, and had a very pleasant supportive wife by his side. He was also very thrifty, to this day spending much of his vacation at the Wellfleet flea market looking for bargains. Like Ned, he often used quaint, nerdy phrases like, "Howdy-doody neighbor."

While Dad and I had prior camping experience, the rest of our family had not. In 1980 I was fourteen years old. Spending a week in a tent with my parents and three siblings ages four, seven, and twelve, would certainly challenge my patience and adaptability, but this challenge was far greater for Mom. The last time my mother slept in a tent in the wilderness was in Yellowstone, August 1971, which left her fearful and tenuous.

At that time, Dad packed us up in his 1967 Chrysler Impala and drove cross-country to explore America's first national park. I was only four years old at the time so most of my memories are those of pictures shown on Dad's slide projector over the years. There are a couple things that still live in my memory banks. I remember visiting the Cody Museum and standing in front of a huge painting of Indians shooting buffalo with bows and arrows from horses. One huge buffalo, riddled with arrows, staggered to its death in a field of tall green grass as painted Indians on white and brown ponies looked on. The other memory from Yellowstone that I keep is the strong smell of rotten eggs produced from sulfuric acid emitted from mud pots and geysers as the Earth's geothermal energy rises from its deep inner core. Other than that, I remember what Dad's Kodachrome slides show.

During that trip to Yellowstone, my parents decided to camp in the park and experience all nature had to offer. Bears have long been uninvited quests to campsites, especially when food is available. My parents have many pictures of people feeding the bears in

Yellowstone, despite the warnings from the park rangers. Dad was excited to photograph such majestic animals but knew to keep his distance, especially when observing a female bear with cubs.

The first night in the park, after eating at our picnic table, my parents cleaned up and placed all the trash in sealed metal "bear-proof" cans. The food was stored in an aluminum cooler with strong metal hinges, left on top of the picnic table. Dad threw dirt on the campfire to extinguish the flame, and we retired to our tent for the evening. Later that evening my parents were awakened as the back wall of the tent was pushed in, knocking the suitcases onto their sides. Realizing that there was no strong wind outside to produce such force, they knew some living beast was outside the tent. At 2:00 A.M., it was unlikely a human, unless they were up to no good. Within minutes, my parents began to hear growling just outside the tent along with loud banging and scratching noises. Dad's heart, now beating out of his chest as sweat appeared on his brow, knew this was no small animal. Hoping to see a group of raccoons, he quietly unzipped the front of the tent and peered outside. Mom sat frozen, holding two sleeping boys—one in each arm. Dad saw nothing in the moonless darkness, but heard noise from the picnic table. He quickly grabbed us kids and ran for the car, Mom following behind whispering, "Richard, what the hell have you gotten us into?"

"I wish I knew, LaVerne! C'mom, get into the car."

With Rob and me wrapped in blankets, fast asleep in the

backseat, Dad started the car and turned the highbeams on. My parents' jaws dropped to see a huge Grizzly bear sitting on top of the picnic table devouring the contents of the cooler. Unfortunately, Dad had left his camera in the tent and was unwilling to go back and retrieve it, for obvious reasons. With each minute my parents spent observing that bear eat their food, Mom's fear of camping rose exponentially. Inside she thought, "What if that bear ate all our food and we remained sleeping? What next? MY CHILDREN!!!"

"Never again, Richard! We are not camping anymore. If you can't see that me and your children sleep in a warm secure place from here on, we might as well drive back to Pennsylvania tonight. Didn't you realize we were in danger? You need to think about your children. Blah, Blah, Blah…"

I know that Dad was grateful that he and his family survived the Grizzly incident unscathed, but I think the tongue-lashing Mom gave him afterward may have been with the same fury of a real Grizzly bear attack. Needless-to-say, the remainder of the trip was spent in hotel rooms or cabins at night, doors locked, and no food left outside. That old aluminum cooler, now mangled from the bear's assault, hinges bent and twisted, rests in my parents' attic as the only reminder of the event, which was never photo documented.

Nine years later, Mom faced her fears, which had given her nightmares since the now famous "Grizzly incident." Dad reassured her that there were no bears on Cape Cod and, therefore, we were all safe and in no danger whatsoever. We would be sharing the wilderness with only friendly animals like foxes, raccoons, opossums, skunks, squirrels, and non-venomous snakes. I don't think this reassured Mom at all.

As we kids crawled out of Dad's truck, Rob and I found no sandy beach to run to as we had done for so many years at Mary Lou's. Here, instead, the ground was covered in dry brown pine needles and fallen leaves. We pulled in front of our campsite, Number Seven.

"Look guys, we've got lucky campsite Number Seven. We're in for a good week," Dad said in an up-beat voice, trying to motivate us, as he saw disappointment in our eyes.

"Where are the bathrooms?" asked Mom.

"There's a central shower facility and bathrooms about 500 yards up that dirt path. Look, here's a map. There are also some job-johnnies scattered throughout the campground. Me and the boys can use that pine tree you're leaning on and not have to walk so far."

"Not funny Richard." Mom was not impressed. Walking a quarter of a mile to go to the bathroom and shower was not what she had in mind when she signed up for this adventure. Reality was starting to set in as she watched Dad construct the tent as Rob and I unloaded the truck, stacking our cargo on the picnic table.

Before long, Phyllis and Emil arrived at our campsite and helped my parents straighten up. We kids disappeared into the piney woods of the campground, chasing chipmunks with sticks as they scampered away, always unscathed. We found blueberry bushes and filled our plastic cups, later to be added to our cereal. After dinner, the trash and food were locked-up in the back of Dad's truck to prevent any further animal attacks.

The first part of the week brought perfect weather: cloudless warm days with little wind. We launched our brown Glasstron easily from the Provincetown boat launch and had no mechanical issues. This week was unusual in that we heard reports of huge schools of mackerel in the harbor, not caught by us here before. Dad spent some time (and money) in Nelson's bait shop to learn the ways of the mackerel and how to catch them. He bought mackerel rigs—long monofilament lines containing six hooks dressed with colorful fluorescent surgical tubing.

With four children on board, Dad located a school of fish under the boat. There were many boats in the area, and birds were diving all around us. Within seconds of striking the water, we hooked, not one single fish, but up to six at a time. There was so much action that Dad became overwhelmed and had to limit the number of rods allowed in the water at one time. Initially releasing the mackerel, all weighing less than a pound, Dad knew that these fish were oily like the bluefish and would not be eaten by our family.

"Daddy, lets keep the fish. I don't want to throw them back," pleaded Kristen.

"Yeah Dad, we can sell them on the wharf to the commercial guys. They use them as tuna bait," said Rob, always looking for a quick buck. "We'll split the profits based on who catches the most fish."

Dad thought for a minute and Fishin' George came to mind. Dad figured if old George could make a profit on vacation doing the thing he loved, why shouldn't we? Now incentivised to catch even more, we filled Dad's live wells with these oily fish. Torpedo shaped, with iridescent blue-green backs, marked by many black stripes, silver-white on the underbelly, the mackerel filled our boat. As the fish now overpopulated our live wells, they lay covering the floor of our boat, creating a thin oily layer of slime.

Finally, we were overwhelmed, and there was no room for more fish. Despite our pleas, Dad, as captain, made the decision to cease fishing for the day. He now tried to master a plan to transport the more than 150 Atlantic mackerel back to MacMillan Wharf and sell them before the heat of the afternoon sun melted their flesh. Leaving the fish where they lay in the boat, he trailored the boat out of the parking lot, stopping at the local hardware store to purchase several plastic containers to contain them along with several bags of ice to cool them, at a cost of about twenty-six dollars. Rob and I argued over who caught the most fish as we thought of things to buy with our profits. We pulled up to the fish processing building on the wharf, and Dad handed over several large plastic containers overflowing with mackerel. A long-haired, black-bearded man wearing dirty yellow rubber overalls weighed each container, added the total on his calculator and handed Dad his stipend.

"How much did we make Dad," we all asked anxiously as Dad loaded the empty containers into the back of the truck.

As he drove off the wharf, Dad began to explain the economics regarding supply and demand. With mackerel that plentiful in the harbor the cost was driven down to next to nothing. While Fishin' George's stripers brought nearly six dollars a pound, Dad's mackerel brought less than six cents a pound, and he was paid $5.42 for the whole lot. Considering the expenses for gas, mackerel rigs, ice, and the plastic containers to transport our catch, we were well into the red for the trip, and there would be no way to recover our losses from mackerel, even if we filled the boat every day. Despite this, I'm sure Dad would not have traded the experience for any amount of money.

We returned from the fishing trip, smelling strongly of dead fish and, therefore, had to shower before Mom would allow us back into the tent. Mom escorted my sisters, Rob, and me up the dirt path to the shower facility. Although clean and well-maintained, the thought of showering in a public place, wearing flip-flops so that your feet didn't contact the floor where others had stepped, and placing quarters in a meter to buy water just gave me the willies. At age fourteen, where modesty is more important than vanity, I struggled to get clean and remain in cognito. We walked back to our campsite carrying wet towels, dirty clothes, and a plastic bag full of soap, shampoo, toothbrushing equipment, combs, and other bathroom essentials. As we traveled back on the dirt path, shivering and still wet-headed, mosquitoes began to attack our tender flesh. With arms full, our only means of defending their strike was to run for the tent, much more difficult to do in our flip-flops than our Converse Chuck Taylor sneakers. Half-way down the path Rob began to increase his pace and challenge me to the finish line.

"Last one to the tent is a rotten egg!" he shouted as he tried to pass on my left.

I looked over my shoulder as he approached and before I could accelerate, my flip-flop caught a tree root that was traversing the dirt path. I immediately fell face first onto the ground with all that I carried strewn all around. Rob fell over me, landing just off the path. Both of us held back the tears, realizing we would gain no sympathy from Mom who by now was carrying both my sisters back to the tent as they cried from the stings of their mosquito bites. Rob and I arrived back at camp, scraped and bruised, with bits of leaves and pine needles enmeshed in our hair. We were likely dirtier now than when we first headed toward the showers. Dad used the ice cold water from the spout of the cooler to wash our hands and face, perhaps to teach us a lesson. After the experience, I concluded that the pleasure of getting dirty just wasn't worth the trouble. We retired into our tent for the evening and, although our accommodations were not comfortable, we quickly fell asleep each night. The sedating after-effects from a beautiful day on the water are far greater than the strongest sleeping pill.

As we emerged from our tent the next morning, Dad had prepared scrambled eggs and bacon on the Coleman stove. Mom opened the cherry-cheese danishes she had brought from home. We listened to the radio forecast as Mom doused us in bug spray.

"Sounds like we got some rain moving in tomorrow, Dad," I said.

"Oh, you know how these weather guys are. They're wrong half of the time. I wouldn't worry about it. Let's just enjoy the good weather today."

Dad tried to minimize the bad forecast, for he needed to keep the morale of his troops high. We decided to rent bicycles and explore the dune trails of the Outer Cape. Throughout the national seashore, miles of paved bike trails offer spectacular views. We drove through oak and scrub pine forests, past marshes, and fresh water ponds. Dad served as tour guide and introduced us to many different plant species, unique to this area. Rose hips and beach plums provide bright-orange, red, and purple accents to the green shrubs on the dunes. When I travel these trails now I appreciate the unbelievable beauty of rolling sand dunes surrounded by a background of deep, blue ocean. Back then, I was more interested in racing my brother down the trail.

The next morning, we awoke to the sound of thunder and falling rain. Unfortunately, the weatherman was correct in his forecast and predicted rain for the next two days. My sisters were too young to understand the implications of bad weather. For me and Dad, it meant no fishing and Mom's mood becoming as foul as the weather. Rob probably saw it as an opportunity to have his siblings confined inside a tent, allowing easy access for torment-ing, as well as an opportunity to visit the shops in Provincetown, where we bought toys and candy, used as bribes for his good behavior. Mom would not see the beach and would be facing the difficult task of maintaining camp, keeping her daughters warm and dry, and preventing Rob and me from killing each other.

As the rain continued, boredom set in. Today, our children are easily captivated and distracted by technological wonders. We cannot travel two miles to Walmart without a DVD movie playing in the backseat of our Suburban. When we vacation, the kids' backpacks are stuffed with Portable Playstations, Nintendo DS's, Portable DVD players, and Ipods, all wrapped in a tangled web of electrical cords and headphones. Back then, our games did not rely on batteries or electrical current. Bolo-bats, find-a-word puzzles, and card games were used by my parents as tools to dis-tract Rob and me from tormenting each other. However, before long, the rubberband strings broke and the bolo-bats were used as weapons. Ultimately, one of us was struck and injured, leading to tears, then tattling. A cascade of events followed, which involved a brief interrogation by Mom to determine who was truly at fault. Rob and I tearfully pled innocence and cast blame on each other. An "accident" was often used to excuse our behavior, as my clenched fist "slipped" into the side of Rob's head, or I "mistakenly" placed my foot in front of Rob's leg causing him to fall face-first into the picnic table. In desperation, knowing we were both at fault, we sometimes corroborated our stories, even blaming our four-year-old sister Kimberly for initiating the altercation. Ultimately, without a clear-cut antagonist, Mom would enforce a truce and threaten to involve my father if we resumed our bad behavior. Dad would certainly be involved if there was any bloodshed on our part, which was fortunately rare.

As the weather became gloomier, so did our demeanor. I awoke the morning of the second day to the continued tapping of rain falling on the canvas tent, now smelling damp and musty. I hoped that I was still asleep and that this nightmare would soon end. Our tent was old and was beginning to succumb to the persistent onslaught of wind and rain. Narrow channels of pooled water began to form along the tent floor, where it met the side-walls. Dad placed rolled towels along the sides of the tent and tried to rally us once more, offering to take us to Tips for Tops'n Restaurant for a hot breakfast of blueberry pancakes and scrambled eggs. We reluctantly agreed—anything was better than sitting in this tent.

"Maybe we oughta head home early," suggested Mom. "It may rain for the rest of the trip, and I don't plan to spend the remainder of my vacation inside a wet tent."

"Relax LaVerne, I bet you the weather clears by this afternoon," said Dad, always the optimist.

After a long breakfast and several cups of hot coffee, we climbed back into Dad's truck and drove through town. We stopped at the Pilgrim's Museum to kill some time. Behind large glass cases were old Pilgrim and Indian artifacts as well as large models of old sailing ships, including a diorama of the Mayflower Compact signing in Provincetown Harbor. I must have been interested in medicine by that time because what struck me most, of all the items exhibited, were the surgical and dental instruments used on ships at that time. Old rusty knives, saws, pliers, and chisels of all sizes were lined up on display. An old bottle of whiskey was always nearby to not only be drunk by the patient to dull his pain, but also poured into the wound as an antimicrobial agent. Patients were given a musket ball to bite on during their surgery, often an amputation. There were numerous musket balls on display that were literally squashed flat in the middle from the force of the sailor's jaw as he mashed his teeth down to endure the pain of the operation. In medicine today, patient comfort is nearly as important as patient safety and outcome, far different than that practiced in the seventeenth century. Now, in practice when I'm having a bad day and listening to difficult patients complain about their severe irritable bowel symptoms or hemorrhoidal itching, I'm tempted to reach into my black bag and hand them a musket ball, in lieu of a pill. Instead, I bite my tongue, think of warm sunny beaches, and move on.

We also stopped by the Marine Specialties store (a.k.a. Army Navy store) in Provincetown. I've not been to many Army Navy stores, but I'm confident that this is probably the most unique. It is certainly the most cluttered store imaginable. As we walked through this dark, long, narrow store on Commercial Street, we quickly became separated. There is no order in this place. The aisles are narrow and cluttered with everything from clothes, both old and new, many used, to dried pufferfish and old ships' anchors. Large bins are scattered throughout the store containing all sorts of shells, starfish, crab claws, and sharks' teeth. Old army surplus uniforms, cans of C-rations, buttons, medals, bullets, belt buckles, and scuba gear are scattered on shelves and hang from the walls. The back of the store features knives, guns, and samurai swords, even an old ship's cannon. Bins containing old posters—everything from World War II to Elvis and the Beatles—document our past. After about an hour of perusing, buying nothing, we rejoined at the front of the store and walked back to the truck.

When we returned to the campground, the rain was still coming down in buckets. As we pulled into "lucky" campsite Number Seven, the tent was sagging in the middle as a newly formed stream was flowing along the side of the tent washing away the sand from around the ground spikes and support poles. Mom and the girls climbed back into the tent as Dad secured the poles once again. Inside, there were new puddles of water and the roof was leaking from two different sites. Mom placed two pots on the floor of the tent to collect the water, which was steadily dripping from the roof.

"I better go check on Phyllis and Emil. Robbie and Ricky, you stay here and help your mother. I'll be back in a little while." Dad marched away in the pouring rain wearing his yellow rubber raincoat and holding a boat cushion overhead to serve as a makeshift umbrella.

In Dad's absence, our sagging tent quickly degenerated into a three ring circus. My sisters, ages four and seven, had brought in some sand in buckets from outside and were now making small sandcastles and mud pies using the water that had leaked inside the tent. Rob had collected a few small frogs in a plastic cup and now was teasing my sisters, threatening to place them in the girls' sleeping bags. The girls screamed at Rob and retaliated by throwing sand across the tent at him. Mom sat on top of a suitcase, face-in-hands, and wept.

I grabbed hold of the pots, now about to overflow with rainwater, and emptied them outside. The flowing water was now within inches of our tent. We were about to lose everything to this flash flood. Back inside the tent, Mom had picked up a large hand-mirror and threatened my brother, as he tied my sister

Kim's pony-tails together in knots. I knew she was at a breaking point; I had to do something. If Mom decided to crush the mirror over my brother's skull, we would not only be dealing with a concussion and scalp lacerations, but also seven years of bad luck. Mom had been known to break a few bolo-bats over Rob's behind, but never a mirror. Regardless of my brother's condition, I couldn't image seven years of bad luck. Although, at times, it seemed as though we had nothing but bad luck, especially on summer vacation.

I erupted from the tent, running quickly to Emil's camper, and pounded on the door. Breathless and dripping wet, I entered the small, warm camper to find Dad and Emil sitting at the table enjoying fresh crab and Heineken.

"Dad, you gotta come quick! The tents about to flood, there's a river approaching, the roof's leaking, the girls have thrown sand all over the tent, Rob released frogs in the tent, and Mom's crying. I'm afraid she's about to go ballistic and kill Robbie." I couldn't get the words out fast enough.

Dad looked at me and looked at Emil. Whenever he receives bad news, he squints. With his facial muscles contracted and fasciculating, nearly shut tight highlighting all the creases, mouth also clenched tight exposing a painful grin, Dad listened intently. As if locked in tetany, Dad squinted harder and longer than I'd ever seen him squint before. Had we been sitting in subfreezing temperature, I'm sure his face would have shattered.

"Emil, thank you for a wonderful lunch. I've got some things to tend to."

Dad put his raincoat over my shoulders, and we jogged back to the tent. As we approached, we could hear the muffled voice of my mother trying to regain control of the situation as she yelled at my brother. We could also see the river now further eroding the foundation of our tent. When we arrived at the campsite, Dad immediately reached into the tent, grabbed hold of Rob's arm, and jerked him outside, dragging him to the truck and placing him in the front seat, slamming the door.

"You stay in that truck and don't move until I tell you. I'll deal with you and your frogs later."

Dad then got Mom and the girls out of the tent and escorted them to Emil's camper, to be fed, warmed, and dried. When he returned, he released Rob from the truck and instructed him to get into the tent, find the frogs, and clean-up all the wet sand from inside. Without a shovel, Dad used a clam rake to construct a trough to carry the approaching water away from the tent. The ground was softened with the rake and then the wet sand excavated with a plastic bucket, ultimately developing a trench about two feet wide. The effects were immediate as the water now flowed away from our tent, and the ground became less saturated.

The inside was cleaned by Rob, the frogs were captured and released, and a small portable heater was placed in the tent. Miraculously, the rain began to ease, and the chipmunks returned from their burrows. The birds began to sing as if to announce a change in the weather. Mom and the girls returned from Emil's camper, now rested and dry. Mom smiled brightly as she entered the warm, clean tent, protected from any further rains. Dad looked over to Rob and winked at him, signaling his cue.

"Mom, I'm really sorry for the way I acted before. I hope you and the girls accept my apology for my awful behavior, and I promise never to do it again." Rob's horns now retracted into his head, and a bright halo emerged. I knew this was all a scripted act written and enforced by Dad, and Mom probably did too.

"I accept your apology, Robbie, and thank you for acknowledging your bad behavior and cleaning up the tent. We'll have to get you a prize in Provincetown tomorrow."

Rob looked over to me with a smirk. I had to leave the tent, for I was about to get sick. Just a few hours ago we were facing total annihilation because of two things—Rob and the weather. Now he's being rewarded for his bad behavior just because he apologized and cleaned the tent. What next, a Nobel Peace Prize? I was the one who went out in the rain to bring Dad back to rescue us. Any thanks for that? None. Some things, and people, just simply go unnoticed. I bit my tongue and was thankful that the rain had stopped.

The next morning, I awoke to see sunlight shining through the mesh window of the tent and heard a full ensemble of birds chirping outside. We emerged from our tent to see a clear blue sky. The smell of the fresh, clean campsite, damp with the morning dew, was really indescribable, but unforgettable once you experience it. A gentle breeze brought simple pleasant aromas of salt air, pine, grass, coffee, and wood smoke, which filled our lungs and made all the bad memories from the days before laughable.

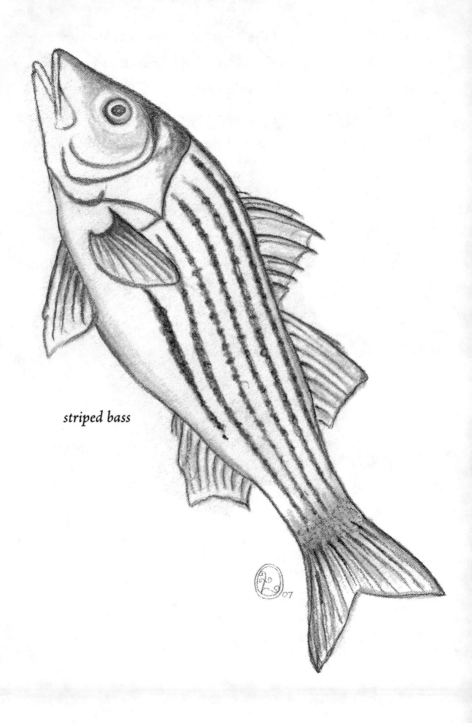

striped bass

Chapter Fifteen

June Stripers

Most Cape Codders feel that September and October are the most enjoyable months on the Cape, offering many good beach days with few tourists remaining. I would certainly agree, but would include June as a close second. While the warm summer weather often extends well into the fall, it hints of its arrival in June, often providing warm, sunny days and cool—wool coat—nights.

In my adulthood, I fully appreciate the peaceful solitude of vacant beaches and empty streets found during this time of the year. Growing up, our summer vacations were always scheduled in July and August, as most are, to coincide with the school schedule. With an economy dependent on tourism, the true beauty and appeal of this place can often be overshadowed by traffic, noise, and crowds arriving in July and August to enjoy it. For these reasons, I would choose June and September. I now face the same school-scheduling restrictions as my parents, still bringing my family here in late July. However, in the past five years I've started a new family tradition whereby those of us with a Y chromosome spend an additional week in June, now referred to as the "guys' fishing trip."

For years, we've heard Uncle Bob refer to June as the best month to fish for stripers on the Cape. He told stories of huge schools of fish arriving from their mid-Atlantic winter estuaries, hungrily pursuing eels, squid, menhaden, and herring. He argued that the stripers were more aggressive this time of year, expending much energy to arrive at their Outer Cape feeding grounds, now needing to replenish their caloric losses. Additionally, they were far less pressured in June than they would be in later summer months. And finally, there were less bluefish around to attack our lures before the stripers got to them.

"I'm going back to my roots," he would say as he planned trips in June, which never came to fruition. "You guys just don't know what you're missing in June, trust me."

In the spring of 2002, I decided to take Uncle Bob "back to his roots" and organized the first "guys' fishing trip" in June of that year. Reserving a beach house was easy and less expensive as there were many vacancies during this off-peak time. The inclusion criteria for those participants were simple: male members of the family who enjoy fishing. Since its inception in 2002, the June trip has nearly been an annual event, regularly attended by three generations of my family (Dad, myself, and my son James), along with brother Rob, Uncle Bob, Uncle Tom, and cousin Tommy, Jr.

For any visitor to the Cape, June offers warm sunny days, often breezy and sometimes cold, with cool nights. For us it offers a chance to enjoy simple things that we have done since childhood. Unlike vacations in later summer, where our wives have made plans for us throughout the week, June has no particular schedule, other than the tides. We depart on Saturday morning, unconcerned about timing our arrival, as Dad's rule of getting through Buzzard's Bay by 8:00 A.M. doesn't apply in June. As we pull into the Pamet River parking lot, I am struck by its emptiness. With only a few boat trailers occupying the lot in what I'm used to seeing dozens of trucks and trailers lined up parallel between white lines, the parking lot appears deserted. Swishy is usually in his shack along the dock next to the boat ramp and often greets us as we prepare to launch.

"Good mornin' gentlemen, you guys here for the week?" he asks, carrying a mug of steaming coffee in one hand and his clipboard in the other.

"Yes, sir. How's the fishin?"

"A little slow last week but the commercial guys have brought in some keepers off Billingsgate Shoal and on the back side. This cold front's supposed to move on this week so you guys should have better luck."

Swishy collected his six-dollar launch fee and handed us our receipt. He, like everyone else connected to the fishing industry on the Cape, fed us what I call the classic fishing scenario. Knowing that we had anxiously waited all year for this week to arrive and wanted to hear good news about the fishing, he told us that the fishing had been slow last week so that we would not be expecting too much and would not be disappointed if we caught nothing. He also stated that the commercial fisherman (a.k.a. the "pros") did fairly well in harvesting some large fish in areas that we were familiar with, so that if we were as good as we thought we were, we, too, should have some luck. Finally, he left us with some hope. Calling for better weather, which would bring more fish, he told us exactly what we wanted to hear. Fishermen are eternal optimists, always hoping for better luck than they've had before, catching bigger fish and more of them. Whenever I asked Dad if he thought we would catch anything on a given day, he would always respond by saying that he wouldn't even consider going if he thought we would not do well. Swishy, as well as every bait and tackle store owner, knows this as well. Fishermen will keep coming back as long as there is hope, and the seed of hope is fertilized by encouraging words from people who are supposed to know what they are talking about. Truth is a different story. Sometimes the truth is modified in order to give us hope, and we all know this. For example, if we arrived to hear Swishy report that no fish were caught in the past month and the weather was calling for gale force winds and heavy rains all week, what would we do? We would certainly be disappointed, but would somehow find a way to wet our lines and fish off the beach in heavy raingear. However, I've yet to arrive and hear a bad fishing report and terrible weather forecast from the experts and bet that I never will.

Before we leave the parking lot at Pamet River, we often place our minnow traps, baiting them with stale bread and dinner rolls. The prey we are pursuing are small fat minnows referred to as mummichugs, which are like candy to fluke and bluefish. In June the water flowing through Pamet River is painfully cold and, therefore, our work must be done from shore. A two-piece cylinder made of wire mesh with inverted cones on either side is baited, clipped shut, and tossed into the middle of the river. A white string secures the trap, and it is tied to a rock on shore, left overnight in the river. The next day, we arrive back in the parking lot, step over the guard-rail that borders it, and climb down the rocky barrier wall to the river. The white string is now covered with thin brown ribbons of seaweed and slimy green moss. With muddy-green spider crabs scurrying away, we pull the trap toward shore. It is heavy with the resistance from the water as it is dragged across the sandy bottom, bouncing off rocks on its way toward shore. As it emerges from the depths, the trap is often boiling with minnows trying to escape their confines. The trap is lifted out of the water, revealing fat brown minnows with white bellies, flopping on a bed of soggy bread, awaiting their transfer into a large bucket, soon to be baited on a hook and drifted to a hungry fluke. For whatever reason, this simple ritual is something I look forward to every year, especially when I can share it through the excited eyes of my children.

The June fishing trip is not without mishaps; however, without women on the trip many of these will go unnoticed and undocumented and soon will be forgotten. Several stories are worthy of retaining and sharing with the other family members. Launching our boat at Pamet Harbor seems easier in June, despite windier conditions. I suspect this is because there are fewer spectators around to bear witness to our follies, not to mention that Dad is now retired from the captain's chair since his maiden launch of *The Watermonkey*, which resulted in near disaster for not only our boat but many other moored boats and dingies in the area (detailed in a previous chapter). Even after this event, Dad was given chances to redeem himself before his demotion. The last straw fell on a June trip in 2004 when we approached the marina. Routinely, we call ahead on channel nine from our ship-to-shore radio and arrange to be taxied to Flyers Marina from our mooring in the harbor. Without fail, a quick response from shore confirms our request, and the boat is secured as we await our water taxi. On this occasion Dad called in over the radio, but got no response.

"This is Captain Rich from *The Watermonkey* requesting a pick-up."

"Come in Flyers, this is *The Watermonkey*, we are requesting a pick-up from our mooring."

Nothing but static returned from Dad's request.

"Flyers, this is your *Watermonkey* captain speaking. We are moored in the harbor, offshore about three hundred yards. We need to be picked-up and brought back to shore. We are on the white mooring next to the blue and white sailboat. Can you hear me? Please, please respond."

Dad became more frustrated with each call to shore, raising his voice so loudly that he likely could be heard on shore without the radio. We were all puzzled, knowing that Flyers Marina was still open and could see employees walking on the dock. We even saw the water taxi bringing other boaters in from their moorings. What was wrong? Did we offend someone? Why were we not being picked-up?

"Are you sure the batteries are working Dad?"

"Just had them replaced yesterday. Listen, I don't know what their problem is, but if we wait much longer, we'll be into dead low tide and will have to walk into shore. I'll drop you guys off on the dock, get some help from a real person on shore, and have them follow me back to the mooring to take me in."

We couldn't disagree or devise a better alternate plan so we disengaged our clip from the mooring as Dad restarted the engine. As we headed into shore, I inspected the radio to find that we had been calling for help on the wrong channel.

"Dad, didn't you know that the marina is on channel nine, not channel eight? No wonder why they didn't answer."

My father acted as if he didn't hear me, but I know he did. Rather than admit his mistake, go back to the mooring, and call for a pick-up on the correct channel, he continued enroute straight to the boat dock. As he neared the dock, we noticed that he was taking a fairly acute angle toward the target, with the bow nearly ninety degrees perpendicular to the dock. In these calm waters with little wind, I would have chosen a softer angle in my approach, to gently pull up alongside the dock and tie a line to a cleat as my passengers jumped out and pulled me securely against the dock. Instead, Dad continued on his direct path toward the dock, with a steady, brisk pace. As we neared our destination, Dad's anxiety got the best of him. Rather than pulling back on the throttle and reversing the motor to slow the boat, he thrust forward on the accelerator and collided directly with the large, wooden piling on the corner of the dock. The contact between our fly-bridge and the dock not only threw us forward in the boat, but lifted the floating dock nearly a foot out of the water. The wake produced by the collision notified those on shore of our arrival as our fly-bridge, now cracked at its origin, stood bent upward at a ninety-degree angle.

After securing the boat and confirming that there were no casualties, with near-mutiny aboard *The Watermonkey*, Dad reluctantly but willingly relinquished his rank as captain. He would continue to serve as co-captain and chief navigator, but would only sit in the captain's chair in open water. The fly-bridge was repaired with epoxy, but to this day remains scarred from the incident.

Even in the best conditions, with an able captain at the wheel, we have had problems. When we arrive in June, as in any other month, we are excited and look forward to launching the boat as soon as possible, often on the first day of our arrival. Our launch is always dictated by the tides as we are unable to launch effectively within two hours of low tide. Several years ago, Pamet River was dredged, which resulted in a wider, deeper channel from the bay into the river to the boat launch. Theoretically, this allows access to and from the launch, even in dead-low tide. Several years ago, in our haste to launch on the first day, we decided to challenge the channel in dead-low tide, even with Swishy's blessing who felt that we would have no problem.

"The commercial guys do it all the time. You should have no problem as long as you keep inside the channel and keep you motor trimmed up."

Foolishly, we decided to take his advice and launch in dead-low tide in order to have our boat on its mooring by the end of the first day. The launch went uneventfully, with Rob in the captain's chair and me as first mate, Dad barked out orders from the stern seat as we slowly pulled away from the dock. The channel was located on our fish finder as we could easily see the contour of the bottom drop off to about six feet deep. From the boat we could also see the red and green buoy markers off in the distance marking the channel on either side. With the motor trimmed-up, a large wake of churned water and sand exploded behind our boat as we headed out to the bay. To our surprise, the channel became shallower and narrower as we headed down the river toward the bay. It became more difficult to steer the boat in the wind as the motor had to be trimmed-up farther, now with the prop nearly breaking the surface of the water, churning more and more sand from the shallow bottom. In water barely over twelve inches deep, we now became shipwrecked in the middle of the shallow river, only 150 yards from the bay. With our deep V-hull firmly embedded in the soft sand below, we had two options. First, we could simply wait on the incoming tide to fill the river and allow easy access into the bay. On the other hand, we could take the matter into our own hands, defy nature's reality and get down the river ourselves, saving about an hour's time. The latter is what we naturally decided to do.

Rob, as captain, demanded that everyone roll up their pant-legs and jump overboard into the river. Dad was designated interim captain and would remain in the boat. The other four mates, Uncle Tom, Tommy Jr., Uncle Bob, and me, jumped into the icy-cold water, now flowing briskly upstream as the tide began to rush back into the river. My bare feet penetrated the soft sand on the bottom, and I quickly became numb from the knees down. *The Watermonkey*, now about 800 pounds lighter and more buoyant, was turned to face the bay. With two of us on either side of the stern, Dad gave the signal to push.

"Come on, you lilly-livered land lubbers, push and get us the hell out of this river!"

We all bore down and pushed with all our might as Dad slammed the throttle, slowly advancing the boat toward the bay.

"Come on boys, put your backs into it. Do you want me to get out there and show you how it's done? Don't make me have to demote you guys down to lowly deck-scrubbers," Dad laughed as he sandblasted us with the spray from his prop and spewed 5000 RPMs directly on us. I'm sure Swishy was smiling as he watched through binoculars as the crystal-clear water in the river was now whipped into an emulsification of sand, saltwater, and seaweed.

Now soaking wet and freezing cold, we thought about accepting Dad's offer to get out of the boat and help. Not only would that remove another 280 pounds from the boat, but would also even the score to have him out here freezing in the river alongside us.

After forty-five minutes of struggling in the channel, the tide finally allowed us to move out into the bay. Dad remained bone dry and warm, wearing his red and black Woolrich coat. The four of us climbed back into the boat, shivering uncontrollably in the June wind, the sky full of gray clouds, refusing to allow any sunlight to warm our bones.

"You guys look like you just had a run-in with the Dungarven Hooper," Dad laughed as we all huddled close behind the cockpit, which allowed refuge from the wind.

As we headed east toward Provincetown Harbor, in fairly rough water with two to three foot waves and many whitecaps on the horizon, the motor began to sputter. Every time the throttle was increased, the motor held back. In fact, we could barely reach trolling speeds on the four-mile run to our mooring, and as we slowly puttered along, many diagnoses were made.

"We have a fuel pump issue, must be clogged," said Uncle Tom.

"You're crazy, I just had the lines flushed and filters changed before we left Wilkes-Barre," barked Dad.

"I think your spark plugs are fouled," replied Tommy Jr., "or it might be your water pump."

"The plugs are brand new, but you're right about the water pump."

Regardless of the problem, we knew it had to be fixed, which was a problem in itself. Not only are repairs at the marina costly, they also take time, which is a precious commodity when you are on vacation for one week. We knew this from many prior interactions with the boatyard over the years. They are always extremely busy and may take a couple days just to evaluate the problem. When a diagnosis is made, treatment recommendations are offered, which also takes time. Ultimately the problem is fixed and you are left with a significant bill, much more than you thought possible. Kinda' like going to the doctor with no insurance.

Ninety minutes later we slowly pulled into Provincetown Harbor, attached our cleat to the ring on top of a large white mooring, and called Flyers Marina for a water taxi back to shore. By this time we had dried in the wind and were covered in a sticky, salty film, which burned our eyes and skin. As he had done many times in the past when arriving on land, Dad began to plead with the owner of the marina, asking him to prioritize *The Watermonkey* as he explained the problem.

"John, listen to me. We go back a long way. You've helped me many times in the past, and I, in turn, have given you a lot of business. We've been faithful customers of yours for many years, always using your moorings, repair services, and even rented boats from you when ours were out of commission. I have to ask you a favor. As you know we are only here for a week, and this is something that is looked forward to all year. I spend many long hours working overtime to provide a vacation for my family and would greatly appreciate if you guys could get to my boat as quickly as possible so we can enjoy our vacation. Blah, blah, blah..."

John had heard this same line thousands of times before from thousands of vacationers who think that they are the only ones on the Cape with a boat problem. They feel that their problem is more important than anyone else's problem and should be taken care of immediately. They are always upset when they find out that there are only a few employees working only Monday through Friday, 9:00 A.M. to 5:00 P.M., and therefore, will not have their boat repaired for several days. John is a savvy old salt who is a shrewd businessman, having inherited the boatyard from his father, passed down for generations. A short, stocky man with a bristly unkempt mustache wearing tortoiseshell reading glasses on the tip of his nose and pencil resting over his right ear, he always has the upper hand. Knowing that vacationers are desperate during these times, he commands high fees. Despite this, John always keeps his word, although never allows himself to get pinned down with specifics.

"Listen, Rich, from what you describe, it could be fouled plugs, water pump, impeller problems, or maybe even the lower unit. Hell, it could be a lot of things. I'll see if I can look at it myself tomorrow and figure out what the problem is. If we have to take it out of the water, we might get to it on Monday afternoon. Now go to the cashier and fill out a work order so we can get started."

Uncle Bob now pulled into the parking lot to drive us back to the beach house and knew something was wrong when he saw Dad conversing with John, both without a smile. We all knew that fishing would be done from the beach for at least the next two days.

The next morning brought warm weather, which led us to the ocean-side beaches, where we were welcomed by grey seals lounging in the water offshore, feeding on freshly caught skate. Their black heads bobbed just above the surface as they devoured their catch. From the surf, we caught several small striped bass on sand eels that morning, as the seals jealously looked on from the water. I photographed my five-year-old son, James, standing proudly holding his surf rod as he battled a keeper bass. Wearing a hooded winter coat, he dragged his catch from the turquoise-gray water onto the beach and jumped for joy as we released the fish back into the surf.

Later that afternoon we decided to rake sand eels in the bay near the mouth of Pamet River. Rather than walking about a mile down the river from the parking lot as we normally do, we decided to take a route not taken before. We would simply drive down the beach over the sand to our designation. Dad's brand-new, maroon GMC Z71 four-wheel drive pick-up truck was the chosen vehicle. Since it was Rob's idea, he was designated to drive. Although beach permits were required to allow access onto certain areas of the beach—in certain seasons—and given to those who were compliant with certain specifications and safety equipment, we felt that these rules don't necessarily apply to our group—on this beach in June—with few people around, and no Environmental Police or wardens in site. We knew the risks of getting stuck in the sand, but felt that was unlikely in Dad's brand-new vehicle with brand-new all-terrain tires. With Uncle Tom and Tommy Jr. pulling up their chest waders in the back of the truck, Rob slowly began to drive down the beach. Initially on packed sand with all four tires engaged, we had good traction and our apprehensions eased. As we continued on, the gentle slope of the beach angled us closer to the bay, now on an incoming tide. As if we were on an icy hill, we slid slowly toward the water. Rob tried to turn and redirect the front tires back up the hill, but was unable to maneuver the truck as the loose, soft sand fell out from under the tires. He tried to speed up, but this propelled us more quickly toward the water. Finally, Rob stopped the truck and sat at the wheel, deep in thought.

He quickly hit the accelerator, causing the wheels to spin, digging in and throwing sand far behind the truck. The ruts created by the spinning tires grew deeper. Dad's patience grew shorter, and his heart rate and blood pressure grew higher as he watched Rob bury his beloved truck.

"Be careful Robbie, if you dig yourself too deep, the weight of the truck will rest on the axles, and then we're buried for sure."

"I know Dad. I'm an engineer, remember?"

Engineer or not, Rob was in a bind. He tried to rock the truck back and forth, with Uncle Bob and me pushing from the rear. To no avail, the truck became more embedded in the sand, axles now within inches of resting on the sand, and water approaching quickly. With each soft rush of approaching waves rising on the beach, Dad's beautiful new prize remained in jeopardy of becoming an artificial reef. He knew that he was facing not only the loss of his truck, but also a fine from the Environmental Police when we were discovered without a beach permit—more than likely both.

Now contemplating the call to 911, we saw an old pickup truck speeding down the beach running in and out of the bay in water nearly as deep as its tires. How could this be? Here we are stuck nearly to the axles in dry sand, and those guys are actually driving into the water. We jumped on top of our truck and waved to the other vehicle for help, and they quickly drove toward us. Three teenage boys pulled up to us and asked what we needed. After explaining our dilemma, the water's edge now ten yards from our truck, all three boys responded simultaneously.

"Let the air out of your tires, man."

We knew that you had to drive onto the beach on soft tires with low air pressure. However, we drastically underestimated how nearly flat the tires needed to be, down to about 10lb psi. As the tires were deflated, the laws of physics once again held true and the flattened tires' larger surface area gripped the sand and pulled us easily to safety, just in the nick of time. The water's edge was literally covering the passenger tires about half-way-up. Dad once again carried his bag of black cats over his shoulder, this time his bag demonstrated a silver lining, and we escaped without a scratch, or a fine.

The next morning, after a huge breakfast of blueberry pancakes at the Tips for Tops'n restaurant in Provincetown, we headed directly to the boatyard. *The Watermonkey* was pulled up alongside the dock, and John's senior mechanic was working on the lower unit of the motor.

"Oh boy, that is not good," Dad murmured under his breath as we approached. He knew that lower unit problems are expensive problems and may also take some time to fix.

"What's the verdict, bud?"

"You got sand everywhere down here in the lower unit and the impeller needs to be replaced. Did you guys bury this prop in the sand? I never saw a lower unit with so much sand in it; that is, without a large crack in the unit. You guys are lucky there's not more damage. I should have you fixed up in a couple hours."

What a relief! We had our boat back on Monday, without a huge bill. We all realized that this was a totally avoidable problem had we simply been more patient and waited an extra hour to launch. No one decided to state the obvious, but we introspectively acknowledged that a valuable lesson had been learned here as it had been on the beach the day before, and we moved on.

The peaceful quiet on the beaches in June also carries over into the water as well. There is relatively little boat traffic compared to July and August where the rips off Race Point seem as congested as the Los Angeles 405 during rush hour. As we leave Provincetown Harbor, traveling parallel to the beaches from Long Point to Race Point, we often see huge schools of stripers. In about twenty feet, the clear water reveals hundreds of gray silhouettes moving close to the bottom. Occasionally, one will turn his belly toward us creating a bright silver flash as if a flashbulb just went off under the sea.

Once we arrive at our destination and are positioned in the strike zone (twenty-five to forty-five feet of water), our trolling reels are unlocked and lures are submerged as the boat slowly pulls forward. With little boat traffic in June, it is not difficult to stay on course within the strike zone. However, later in the year, with many more boats including those chartered by customers to produce fish, it becomes more problematic. For the commercial charter captain whose livelihood depends on satisfied clients, smiling and holding up large fish for photos, this is serious business. They pay little attention to vacationing tourists in smaller boats and remain in the strike zone at all costs. This means that if you are a conscientious captain (usually in a smaller boat), you will yield to them as they troll in-between lobster pots, remaining in twenty-five to forty feet of water. If you choose to ignore them, you risk having lines crossed and cut, not to mention a verbal dialogue full of four-letter expletives for having "cut him off."

The strike zone is fairly wide, usually about fifty to seventy-five yards, as the bottom drops off dramatically from twenty to 120 feet offshore. This zone where fish travel to feed would be much more accommodating to boat traffic if it were not for the lobster pots that also are placed within the strike zone. Creating a random maze on the surface in this area are multicolored buoys tethered to ropes, marking lobster traps resting on the bottom, forty feet below. Some say that the bait in the traps provides strong scent, which attracts the fish to these areas.

The lobster trap, with its colorful buoys floating on the surface above, has been a symbol of Cape Cod life for centuries, not only functioning as a source of revenue for lobstermen, but also providing art to the landscape. With the actual traps stacked alongside a cottage, or the lobster buoys hung from a post on the beach, they represent traditional New England art. Regardless of their contribution to the fishing or their artistic value, for me, they represent a challenge to negotiate when trolling three or four lines a couple hundred yards off the back of the boat. When there are large numbers of boats fishing this area, the problem becomes exponential. I recall many frustrating times when I was behind the wheel trying to keep the boat in our desired depth, angling in-between lobster buoys in strong wind and current, looking out for oncoming boats, diving birds, and fish on the sonar.

"How deep are we, Ricky?" Dad would ask.

"We're in thirty-five feet."

"Perfect, perfect. I can smell 'em. Hold on boys, get ready."

Two minutes later, without a strike Dad would ask, "How deep are we, Ricky?"

"Eighty feet, I had to veer off to avoid the lobster pots."

"No good, no good. We'll never hook up out here."

This is a recurring conversation for years. Dad has become the proverbial back-seat boat driver whose comments are often infuriating to those of us trying to maneuver the boat. Since he lost his captain's license because of his inability to remain calm around boat launches and docks, often hitting the panic button as well as other structures in the vicinity, Dad's comments have become more frequent and condescending. I suspect this is because he knows that he'll not be asked to take over the controls and face the same obstacles as we, unless we are in open water. So he is free to mouth off with impunity while we struggle to maintain our position over fish.

Drifting with rigged eels or soft plastic baits through the lobster pots is much easier, with less risk of hooking a pot and losing our rigs. This is often the chosen method of fishing when there is little current and plentiful fish in the area. Drifting on a sunny, warm, breezy June day with the fishfinder chirping is as sweet as the Nora Jones' ballad playing through the speakers of our stereo.

Every now and then Dad's remarks come back to bite him, and we all have a laugh at his expense. Sometimes we even have the good fortune of documenting the event on film. One such episode occurred among the lobster pots off Race Point on a blustery day in June. We had been trolling with great success, having boated several keeper bass within a short time. The water was rough that day, which often activates the fish into feeding mode. Dad, sitting in the stern seat behind the captain's chair, held his trolling rod over the side, pumping it to and fro to stimulate a strike. He was wearing khaki work pants and long-sleeve shirt, with shirt tails hanging out of his pants. The left breast pocket was bulging with a sunglass case, pocket knife, tide chart, fishing hooks and lead weights. His shirt, relatively clean initially, would become stained with coffee, sunblock, and fish blood throughout the week. An Orvis cap with a long, black beak, protecting him from the bright sun, completed Dad's fishing outfit. This cap has been blown off his head numerous times in the wind when traveling at high speeds, each time recovered in our fishing net, no worse for the wear.

As we trolled, large waves crashed over the gunwale, soaking my father again and again with cold ocean water. Knowing that I had little control over the angle at which the waves struck our boat, and certainly no ability to affect the size of the waves, he sat silent, but expressed a tight, purse-lipped, eye-squinting grin on his face that clearly made us all aware how he felt. I did my best to keep him dry, but my best wasn't doing much good. And his khaki clothes were now darker brown, soaked with salt water.

"Rich, you ok over there?" asked Uncle Tom. "You look like you've had a run-in with the Dungarven Hooper. Come on, take the pain."

We laughed as Dad was now receiving what he had been dishing out all week. Suddenly, Dad's arms were ripped back towards the motor as the reel began to scream.

"Whoo, fish on, fish on! Cut the motor!" he yelled as the line continually left the reel.

Dad struggled to his feet as the thick trolling rod bent nearly in half. I cut the engine as we now drifted helplessly in the current. Dad had to kneel back on his seat in order to maintain his balance. The reel screamed relentlessly and would not allow him to regain any line.

"This is no candy-ass fish, boys. Uncle Bob, you may be back at your roots, but I'm about to dethrone you as striper king."

Uncle Bob looked on and smiled. With teeth showing through locked jaws, he acknowledged that whatever was on the end of Dad's line was huge and heavy, and regardless of the species, would certainly overtake the family record.

"This is no small fish, boys. Whew. Oh boy. He's taking line! He's taking line!"

Dad struggled with the giant and continually gave line to the beast. Perhaps he hooked a small tuna, unusual for this time of year. As Dad's line was nearly completely stripped from the reel, we decided to bring the boat back toward the fish. The motor was restarted and thrown into reverse. As we backed into the current following the path of the line, large waves crashed over the stern, soaking us repeatedly.

"I don't care if I have to jump overboard and swim to it, I'm landing this fish."

With boat in gear, Dad was able to regain some line, and it gradually became apparent that the beast at the other end was not moving very much, if at all. We approached the point where the line entered the water and held the boat here. With back-breaking force, Dad pulled hard on the sixty-pound test monofilament line. As he did, a long rope appeared from the depths as a lobster buoy began to approach our boat. We grabbed hold of the buoy and pulled the rope into the boat revealing Dad's lure embedded in the rope about half-way down. Dad's face showed disappointment, shaking his head as we recovered his lure from the lobsterman's rope.

"Nice job, Rich. You now own the record for the largest lobster pot caught on *The Watermonkey*. Take a bow," Uncle Bob laughed as I hit pause on the video camera, documenting this event for posterity.

"Don't worry Uncle Bob, your day will come."

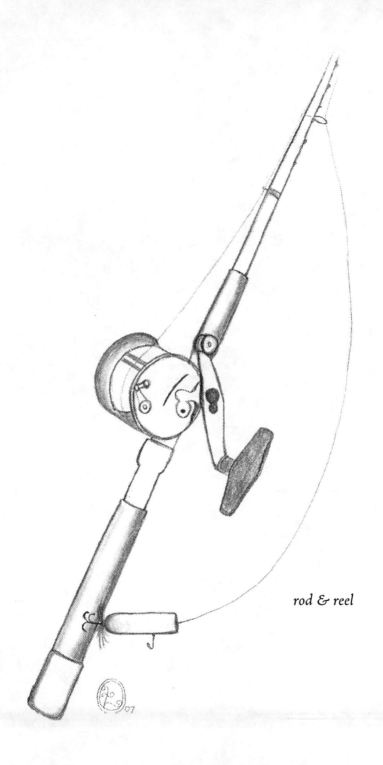

rod & reel

Chapter Sixteen

The Record

Dad's prediction became reality later that summer when Uncle Bob's striped bass record of over twenty years fell to my sister, Kristen, as she boated a thirty-five pound bass on a pink, soft plastic bait drifted in that same area.

It was a hot, humid late-July day with very little breeze to keep us safe from the green-headed horseflies. Dad and I had taken my sisters, wife, and kids out for a boat ride in the bay. Because the water was calm, we decided to venture out into the ocean to show the kids the backside beaches. My daughter Madisen, age eight, sat proudly on my lap, steering wheel clenched tightly in her hands, as she drove us past Wood End lighthouse. As we headed toward Race Point, my son James, age six, but now a two-year veteran of the June "guys fishing trip," told stories of fish he caught from the very waters we were now passing over. In the distance, we saw the familiar image of fishing boats dotting the flat horizon where sky meets ocean. Unlike June, where their numbers are few, more and more boats appeared as we neared our destination.

We counted nearly fifty boats, most of which were trolling through the lobster pots, trying to stay positioned in twenty-five to forty-five feet of water. We laughed as we saw several boats doing battle with lobster pots, as Dad had done earlier that year. As we watched other boats catch fish as terns splashed all around us, our fishing instincts took over, and we decided to wet a line. Rather than struggle with the boat traffic weaving between the pots in the strike zone, we decided to simply shut off the motor and drift in the current along the beach, which favorably carried us along, parallel to the shore.

We decided to drift four rods, each baited differently. I handed my sister, Kimberly, a rod baited with sand eels. Dad tossed a live eel off the back of the boat and placed the rod securely in the rod holder. He then reached into his tackle bucket and pulled out a brown paper bag that was damp and torn. Inside was a plastic bag containing dozens of pink, soft plastic baits resembling the shape of a thin cigar. He tied a jighead to the line and then carefully pierced the tip of the soft plastic bait and secured it to the hook, handing the rod to Kristen.

"Dad, I like your choice of color for the bait, but I don't think the fish have that much fashion sense. Don't you think a more natural-looking color would work better?"

"These Pink Gummies are the very best, Kristen. I overheard

some of the striper fishermen talking at the Goose Hummock Shop. They murdered 'em on these gummies. Pink is the hot color this year, don't ask me why. They are totally deadly!"

My father sealed the plastic bag and placed it back into the bucket before he reeled in his own line to check his eel. I stood on the bow and tossed surface plugs toward diving birds, catching several small bluefish and allowing my children to help reel them to the boat.

As the afternoon progressed, we caught many fish, mostly small stripers and blues. It was about half passed three, with a high sun and a dead low tide, at a time when most fishermen would be doing other things but fishing. While we were relaxing in the sun, now more interested in making plans for dinner than actually catching dinner, Kristen called for help. She had been casting and jigging Dad's deadly pink gummy for nearly two hours without a strike—until now.

"I think I have a fish on, guys," she stated very matter-of-factly, as we watched her rod bend over the rail off the starboard side of the boat. "It feels like dead weight."

"You're stuck on the bottom," barked Dad from the back of the boat. "Hand me the rod and I'll get it free."

Whatever Kristen was stuck to on the bottom was slowly and steadily moving away from the boat, nearly pulling her over the side as she followed the line now heading toward the back of the boat.

"Set your drag, set your drag! You'll lose everything if you don't loosen your drag!" Dad yelled, now realizing that she was not stuck, but was likely battling a huge fish.

I ran over to Kristen and turned her drag counter clockwise to take some tension off the rod and allow the fish to take some line. As the battle ensued, the fish stayed deep, signaling to me that this was likely a large striper, as a bluefish would have surfaced by now, jumping wildly out of the water to spit the hook.

Surprisingly, the fish began to tire fairly quickly, allowing Kristen to regain line that she had initially lost.

"Don't horse 'em, don't horse 'em!" Dad yelled from the back of the boat. These words were spoken hundreds of times before, as words of encouragement/advice given by many male members of my family as they watched other members of the family do battle with fish of all species. If the fish was lost before being boated, gaffed, or netted, the response was then, "See that, I told you not to horse 'em," as if horsing them was something you intentionally tried to do. If the fish was landed successfully, one would often hear, "Good job, see what happens when you don't horse 'em."

In any event, Kristen did not horse 'em, and slowly brought the beast toward the surface. We all stood and stared into the water as a dark back with silver sides slowly revealed itself, wearing a pink gummie embedded in its lower jaw. I was awestruck to see such a large striper approaching my boat, its dorsal fin now breaking the surface of the water. I thought back to the days with Fishin'

George at Mary Lou's cottages and what it must have been like to catch thirty or more of these majestic beasts in one evening on the beach.

I reached over and firmly gripped her lower lip with my thumb, feeling her powerful head shake one last time before lifting her into the boat. Dad's eyes were as wide open as his mouth and, for the first time in history, he was utterly speechless.

"Big striper, big striper!" was all he said.

The fish was quickly measured at thirty-four inches, weighing thirty-five pounds, with a fat belly and thick tail whose circumference was twice that of my hand's grip. Photos and video were taken for the family record book, and the fish was then revived and released back into the depths off Race Point. The fishing was over for the day. Kristen had now accomplished what my father and uncles had dreamed about for thirty years—she hooked and landed a huge striper in the most famous striper waters in North America.

Dad remained relatively speechless. "Congratulations, Kristen, you handled that fish very well. See what happens when you don't horse 'em. I can't wait to see the look on his face when I tell Uncle Bob that he's been dethroned as the striper king."

Later that evening we gathered in the living room, connecting the video camera to the television to replay the event for those who were not there. As everyone watched in disbelief as the fish was pulled from the water and congratulated Kristen on her accomplishment, Uncle Bob was unwilling to concede his title, which he's held for nearly thirty years.

"I hate to tell you guys that the title remains in my hands. You see, in order to claim the record, the fisherman must own the rod that was used to catch the fish. In Kristen's case, the rod was owned by her father, and, therefore, the record is not valid. Period. End of story."

Despite his strong arguments as to why the record holder must own their equipment (which is beyond the scope of this chapter), Uncle Bob failed to convince anyone that Kristen should not hold the title. After a debate that spilled over well into the early morning hours over many adult beverages, and remains contested by Uncle Bob to this day, Kristen remains the newly crowned Striper Queen. Period. End of Story.

starfish

Chapter Seventeen

Commercial Street

Commercial Street is the main artery in Provincetown, running for three miles parallel to the harbor. Home to over 400 businesses, it serves as the focal point for most activities, whether it is shopping, dining, dancing, or just strolling through town and people-watching; it can all be found along Commercial Street. Many old, beautiful homes and colorful gardens also line the street, especially toward the west end of town. Formerly the impressive homes of wealthy sea captains and merchants, many have been converted into shops, restaurants, art galleries, and inns. However, most are well-preserved and maintained in their historical perspective and uniqueness. A wide variety of architectural styles such as Victorian, Gothic, and Greek Revival, to name a few, are all demonstrated here. I once heard Provincetown described as an onion of culture. By peeling back the layers, you find an interesting collage of artists, writers, musicians, business owners, craftsmen, and fishermen, of varied religious, political, and sexual orientation. The root of this onion is Commercial Street.

Although Provincetown was incorporated in 1727, it had no formal streets for over 100 years. Sandy narrow paths connected homes to school, church, and the harbor. Initially, there was significant resistance to building the first street in Province-town in 1835, publicly referred to as a "senseless extravagance." After heated debate, a one-way, narrow street was constructed and named Front Street. Ten years later, after more debate and protest a narrow sidewalk was added to one side of the street, which most pedestrians refuse to use to this day.

Now renamed Commercial Street, it remains twenty-two feet wide as it was in 1835, although paved and bustling. Un-like Pamet River, passively meandering through tidal marshes connecting ocean to bay, Commercial Street is a river of human current; active, dynamic, and erratic, flowing vigorously both east and west, although allowing automobile traffic passage in only one direction.

When driving a vehicle in this human river, you quickly realize your unimportance, more a nuisance than a threat to the thousands of careless humans giving life to this river. Entrance from a side street is granted by the occasional traffic cop who briefly restrains the flow. We have spent many hours—which should have been minutes—making our way through the current, often with boat-in-tow, on our way down Commercial

Street to the Provincetown boat launch. I often feel like the captain of a barge slowly making its way through an iceberg-laden Arctic sea, watching the human obstacles part in front of my bumper, barely avoiding contact. This experience is not for the impatient or short-tempered, as Dad has learned over the years. Revving engines, loud horns, squealing brakes, and intimidating personal threats offer no advantage here.

Commercial Street is a playground for the eccentric, where eccentricity is often the norm. It is the ultimate place for people watching, but most of us who frequent this place don't act as if we notice even the most unusual pedestrians. Elderly tourists arriving on buses from the Bible Belt shuffle along next to long-haired skate boarders sporting baggy clothes, tattoos, and body piercings. Families, both heterosexual and homosexual, push baby strollers while bicyclists weave in and out. The older folks will often sit on park benches under shade trees, watching street performers—magicians, folk singers, and musicians—while men in drag wearing pink tights and lime-green leotards scoot by on roller skates.

My family **has** literally spent hundreds of hours strolling along Commercial Street visiting restaurants, ice cream and candy stores, **shell** shops, clothing stores, kite shops, hardware stores, art galleries, aquariums, and the Marine Specialties store. We've had funny caricatures drawn and faces painted. Marcus Smith, an artist whose studio is a four-foot-wide covered space in between two other buildings along the street, has created beautiful portraits of our children in charcoal and pastel. His gifted hands have preserved, forever in time, faces at ages we will never get back, other than in memories.

I don't think you can write a book about vacation adventures to this area without mentioning another large part of the Provincetown culture—its gay and lesbian community. As the town evolved from a fishing and industrial community to one of arts and tourism, its population also changed, now home to many homosexual couples, its streets crowded with gay tourists in the summer.

To be gay or straight, in my opinion, is not a choice. I believe that there is some yet undiscovered gay gene or protein that makes that choice for us. The choice is that of our actions and behavior once we realize who we are. Commercial Street, at night, demonstrates the many choices people can make. Walking along the crowded thoroughfare, the first-time visitor to this area is often struck by the sheer numbers of men and women walking hand-in-hand and arm-in-arm with their partners. Most of the men are well-dressed and good looking, often described as "eye candy" by the female members of my family.

Most choose to act in a manner that we would all consider fairly normal and appropriate, such as quietly walking along enjoying the sights. Others choose to draw attention to themselves, fulfilling some stereotypes. Therefore, the first-time visitor will also see muscular men in black leather pants, vest, gloves, and cap, walking their Doberman Pincers down the street. Female impersonators and men in drag will be out, some handing out fliers for the evening's cabaret performance. Many will not be noticed as female impersonators—they look that good. We have seen Barbara Streisand, Cher, Tina Turner, Diana Ross, many times over the years, just to name a few. Mom, my aunts, sisters, and cousins still enjoy going to the gay bars at night to enjoy a Karaoke performance by the men in drag. It's all in good fun and usually harmless.

Aside from the occasional "breeder" comment yelled to us from a group of drunken homosexuals, we've had hardly any negative interactions through the years. In college, I often brought friends along to share in our vacation. Many times at night in bars, we would be approached by women when they noticed us looking over at them. Their initial question was always the same. "Are you guys gay?"

"NO!" we would respond emphatically.

"OK, then let's dance."

At that stage in our lives, we were well-tanned, well-groomed, trim, testosterone-laden, horny coeds. How could anyone even think that we could be gay? We would rationalize the interaction by acknowledging that most of these gay guys were also good looking, muscular specimens, so it seems to reason that the women might be curious. Besides, we were never approached by gay men in these bars.

I remember vividly in the late 1980s through the 1990s, when AIDS was a short-term, fatal disease, leading to severe muscle wasting, weight loss, and disfigurement. At that time I was studying the disease in medical school and caring for those patients during my residency. Walking through the streets of Provincetown at that time, it was easy for me to identify those men with AIDS. Skinny, weak, and often alone, many had already lost their partners. Over the past several years, through the miracle of science and modern medicine, HIV has thankfully become a chronic, manageable disease. As evidenced by Magic Johnson, those infected with HIV who can afford the medicine can look forward to a relatively normal, healthy life. This has become manifest in Provincetown, where it is now uncommon for me to be able to pick out an AIDS patient from those walking down the street.

Over the years, I've seen the reactions of first-time visitors to this area vary, depending on their religious, moral, and political convictions, which have ranged from disbelief, humor, anger, or disgust to acceptance, tolerance, and coexistence. Our family has chosen acceptance, with a little humor sprinkled in.

As a child, I'm sure my parents were challenged and uncomfortable in explaining to me why those people were holding hands and showing so much affection for one another. But my parents did it in a way that showed that they didn't condone it, but accepted it as part of this place and that people are not all the same and that we are lucky to live in a country that is tolerant and free. They didn't use those exact terms, but their message of tolerance, acceptance, and coexistence has been consistent throughout the decades, as it should be. There's plenty of room in this place for everyone to enjoy.

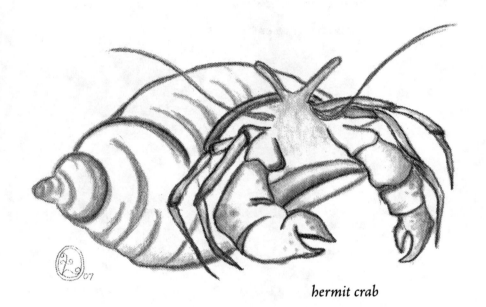

hermit crab

Chapter Eighteen

Sunsets and Shooting Stars

The Outer Cape hasn't changed much in the last thirty-five years. Job opportunities, affordable housing, illegal immigrants, and the delicate balance between human occupation and the preservation of endangered species have become more important issues over the years. We have certainly seen more privatization of property and some moderate residential home development in Truro over the years. But compared to other East Coast beach communities, and because of the national seashore, this area has been spared the ravages of commercialization.

Many of the bayside rental cottage communities along Route 6A, including Ozzie's Ocean Breeze and Mary Lou's Little Skipper, have been sold as condominiums and are no longer available to summer renters. A few years ago, while on the "guys fishing trip" in June, we stopped by the Little Skipper to say hello to Mary Lou, who we hadn't seen in over twenty years. Now a frail, gray-haired old woman, she still remembered our family, even bringing up the squid incident when prompted by my father. She walked us down the clamshell driveway, along the wooden sidewalk where Fishin' George would display his stripers. The old cottages along the walkway looked the same, a bit more faded and not as well-kept by their new owners. At the end of the way, where the wooden planks met the beach, there was now a driveway leading across the beach and down to the bay. Fishin' George was now the owner of the last two beach houses and with the deeds to the houses, came ownership of the beach, all the way to the high tide mark. He now drove his truck onto the beach and launched his boat form here, directly into the bay, avoiding the wait at the boat ramp altogether. This would have never been allowed before and, to me, just didn't seem right.

Mary Lou walked us through the beach house that we used to call home so many years ago. As we stepped on the creaky wooden floors, that familiar smell of old antique wood, Pine-Sol, and bleach brought back pleasant memories. It amazed me how small the house actually was. It seemed so much larger back then. We walked from room to room, ducking under the doorways to avoid banging our heads, and entered the narrow kitchen lined on both sides with old knotty pine cupboards.

"This one's back on the market, if you guys are interested," said Mary Lou.

"What are you asking?"

"$400,000—firm," she said matter-of-factly.

"We'll think about it and get back to you," replied my father, reminded of a similar conversation thirty years ago.

In the mid nineteen seventies, my grandfather, Pop Seidel, inquired as to what Mary Lou would consider selling the very same beach house, as he loved the place and thought about owning a home on the Cape. At that time, Mary Lou responded "$31,000—negotiable."

Pop Seidel's response was, "Mary Lou will have a beard down to her toenails before she gets $31,000 for that beach house. That is simply highway robbery."

Needless to say, thirty years later, the value of this same property has risen nearly 1300%. Pop was a musician, not a real estate investor.

Mary Lou walked us out onto the deck overlooking the beach with the bay off in the distance. Old white wooden recliners and Adirondack chairs lined the deck, probably the same ones that we used to sit on years ago, telling stories late into the evenings on cool summer nights.

"I must have seen dozens of shooting stars from this deck over the years, Mary Lou."

"I've seen thousands, Richard. I hope to see thousands more."

"I don't know what I like better, watching sunsets over the bay, or seeing shooting stars."

"Doesn't matter, Richard, as long as you're seeing them. That's what counts."

From Mary Lou's deck we had watched many beautiful sunsets. Each dusk demonstrating different shades of light and color. As the red sun falls into the sea, the surrounding sky's personality ranges from neon, tangerine, and pink to pastel shades of lemon, lavender, and rose. Later, on a clear, dark night with no city lights to interfere, the black sky lay silent, but alive with a billion stars. A bright yellow moonbeam often illuminates the water. On any given night, as we sat wrapped in a blanket on Mary Lou's deck, if we looked hard enough, we would see a star fall out of the sky.

"Give Fishin' George our best," Dad waved as we pulled out of Mary Lou's parking lot and onto the highway.

Several years ago, Rob and I began to look at properties to build our summer home, as we had talked about since high school. With some perseverance, negotiation, and the help of a local realtor, we found the perfect lot. High on a hill overlooking the bay, a short walk to the beach, with panoramic views of Pamet Harbor and Provincetown, and within walking distance of the Whitman House, it seemed like an ideal spot. Mom will now have her own private bedroom, air conditioning, and a gourmet kitchen; never again having to deal with leaky tents and crowded cottages. Dad will have a large garage to house *The Watermonkey*, store his gear, and hopefully keep his chaos organized.

As we go forward, my hope is to create more pleasant memories with my family from this spot. My children's experience will certainly be different than mine, with exposure to better vehicles, boats, and fishing equipment. I hope that their underlying sense of discovery and joy brought from the sheer natural beauty of this place will keep them coming back for future generations, so that we can share a thousand more sunsets and see a thousand more shooting stars.

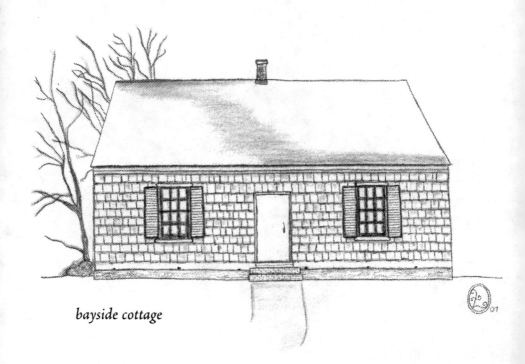

bayside cottage

Photo Memories

Pop, Nana, Ricky, Rob, and Mom at Coast Guard Beach, 1973

Dad's truck with boat-in-tow, 1980

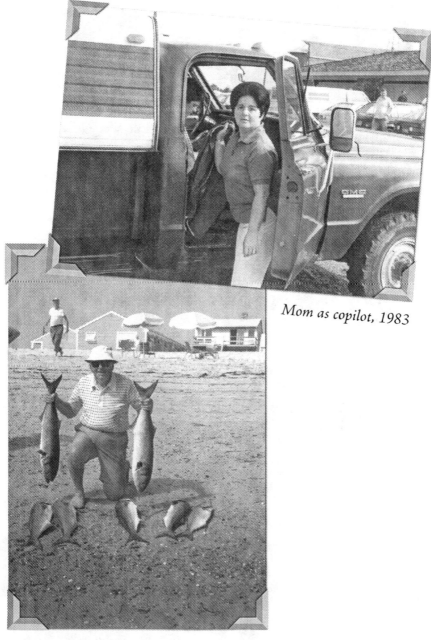

Mom as copilot, 1983

Pop with his trophy bluefish on Ozzie's beach, 1974

My family at Mary Lou's, 1979

Kristen holding her trophy bluefish, 1979

*Captain Pop at Ozzie's showing his blues
with Rob looking on, 1973*

Pop dressed for an evening on the town, 1974

Dad and his gang, 1979

Uncle Tom, Aunt Carolyn, Tommy Jr.,
and Jennifer at Highland Light, 1983

Pop with a lobster ready for the boilin' pot at Mary Lou's, 1980

*Aunt Melinda, Laura, Uncle Neil, and David
on the dune trails, 1980*

Aunt Carolyn, Uncle Tom, and Jennifer at the bayside beach, 1979

Ricky, Kim, Kristen, and David at Mary Lou's, 1978

Jennifer, David, and Laura at Highland Light, 1979

Aunt Melinda, Uncle Neil, Laura, and David
at Highland Lighthouse, 1979

Bailing out the old brown boat.
Dad, Uncle Tom, and me, 1978

Pop and me at Pilgrim Lake, 1972

Dad inflicting a "tin ear", 1980

Rob and Kristen proudly showing their fluke, 1978

Mom and Kim on the dunes, 1977

*Pop and me with the lobster
that destroyed Ozzie's refrigerator, 1973*

Dad with a nice striper, 1974

Fish on! Rob battling a bluefish, 1979

Uncle Bob about to dig in, 1980

Mom and Dad at Ozzie's beach, 1973

Cousins—Kim, Laura, David, and Kristen, 1978

*Kristen, Mom, Kim, Laura,
and Aunt Melinda at the bay, 1978*

Fishin' George's stripers, 1978

*Mom and Madisen at
Head of the Meadow Beach, 2001*

*Aunt Margie and
Uncle Carl, 1998*

*James guards his surf rod
at Race Point Beach, 2002*

Kristen, Madisen,
and Melanie
at Balston Beach, 2001

Tommy Jr. shows off his stripers
on The Watermonkey, 2004

*Madisen and Mom
at Balston Beach, 2002*

*Mark, Drew, and Kim
on MacMillan Wharf, 2005*

Kristen and Doug, 2005

Robert, William, Trish, and Mitchell
in the beach tent, 2005

Welcome to Commercial Street, "Cher" 2005

Cousins, 2004

*Uncle Bob, Uncle Neil, and Dad
on* The Watermonkey, *2004*

Madisen and her prize fluke, 2000

Rob on The Watermonkey, June 2004

Uncle Bob weighing in
another striper
on The Watermonkey,
June 2003

Dad and his
bluefish, 2005

Dad—Undisputed Sea
Robin Champion, 2004

Three generations on The Watermonkey, *2002*

Dad and a nice Race Point striper, June 2004

Uncle Neil, Aunt Melinda,
Aunt Carolyn, and Uncle Tom, 2004

Kristen's record, 2004

Rick and Melanie at Race Point Beach, 2006

Jack's first Cape Cod summer, 2007

Printed in the United States
130324LV00003B/4/A

9 781583 852187